Children of the Air

THE
MOTTLED
SPECK

©2020 Mark Eddy Smith
ISBN: 978-1-939636-04-1
Feather image: iStock.
markeddysmith.com

This is a work of fiction. Any similarity between the characters herein and you or another person, living or dead, is kinda what I was going for.

*For my parents,
without whose gracious generosity and hospitality
this book might never have grown up.*

and

For all who have shared their pain with me.

Winter, Part 1

1.

In her dream, she is always falling, alone in a grayness like mist; the wind, that strong, sustaining spirit, has forsaken her wings.

Endlessly she plummets toward the unseen ground, and the speed increases and the terror swells until she recalls this has happened before. Accepting her fate, she starts to relax, till the mist parts precipitously upon a tumble of stones, smooth and round and white. An instant before impact, she recognizes

Corwynn jerked awake, secure in her aerie, the eggs beneath her miraculously unshattered. Beside her slept Kyron, his head tucked beneath one wing. A cold breeze reassured her of its presence as, across the valley, the late winter sun hesitated behind the line of distant hills.

She stood—awkwardly straddling her eggs—and stretched every muscle, arching her back and spreading her wings. The world behind her was upside-down—untenable—with snow clinging to the undersides of pine boughs whose bottoms pointed skyward. She glared at it for as long as she could, trying to will some of the tension from her joints.

At last she recomposed herself, righting the world, and contemplated the possibility of the wind not simply falling silent and still but being altogether absent, refusing to respond to lung or wing. It was unthinkable: as soon imagine trees turned to rocks, or the mountain to a fish, flapping and gasping in search of the sea. Yet every night the dream returned. Each morning she reflected on its impossibility, until the memory faded with the rising of the sun. She shook her head to hasten its departure and turned her attention to the day.

Although the sky was clear, a far-off thunder rumbled.

· · ·

Kyron awoke to a rumble of thunder that, instead of dwindling, grew louder, repeating its single syllable ever more insistently until the din aroused him completely and he looked up to behold a hideous, oddly-winged monster buzzing toward him. He had seen such things before, gliding across the sky like swollen dragonflies, but never had one approached him. He cowered, hoping a gust of wind would blow it away or that at least it would fly past the aerie without pausing. His wings urged him to follow Corwynn, whose flurry of flapping was quickly overwhelmed by the monster's clatter, but he couldn't help remembering that none of his children yet had wings.

At last, it was hovering directly overhead, and Kyron's bowels emptied. The creature's roar was deafening; its breath a hurricane. It was unmistakably a dragonfly of unimaginable proportions. He raised his wings and screamed but knew, as he did, how small and insignificant he was in comparison. As small and insignificant as a field mouse that squeaks in alarm when he himself descends. Clearly his position was hopeless, but he would not, for that reason, lose hope. Gathering all his strength, he launched himself at what he hoped was a soft underbelly.

It was not. He struck with a resounding boom that echoed even over the sound of the monster's wings, and then he dropped, stunned, back into the nest. A web like a spider's dropped from the monster's side, and Kyron scrambled to cover the eggs with his wings. Glaring up at the hulking insect, he considered grabbing the web and flying hard to jerk the beast out of the sky, but something shadowy emerged from its side and, with a tiny flash, sent a smaller insect hurtling toward him. It struck his back with a sting sharper than any wasp's.

Mind-bendingly, the shadow form shifted, contracting and expanding into the shape of a four-legged creature that crawled from the monster's belly and slowly descended the web.

As the sting's venom overwhelmed him, he saw that, beast or not, the creature reaching toward him had the eyes of an insect, and in those eerie circles he saw another eagle defending a similar nest. Before he lost consciousness, he noted with grim satisfaction that, although the other eagle looked sleepy, he also looked defiant, and not the least afraid.

* * *

Corwynn stared as the dragon shrank into the distance, her beak agape as if she would ask some question of the empty, tactless sky.

He had fought.

While she had flapped away in terror, Kyron had stood his ground.

He who was a giant among eagles, who had carried sheep to his nest to feed his love, who had broken the backs of rams and lifted goats into the sky with the strength of his wings, had defended their aerie to the last, and, though his strength was as a butterfly's before the whirlwind, he had spread his wings over their eggs, and he had triumphed, in a way, for all three of them remained.

Corwynn stood over her round, smooth stones and wept, after the manner of eagles, with her head bowed and her eyes closed.

2.

THE SENSATION IN THE PIT OF LISSY PEABODY'S STOMACH WAS MORE GUILT than fear. As she watched the toboggan slide downhill without her, she could hear her mother's voice: "I *told* you," while she, still in a sitting position, floated toward the bracken on the left-hand side of the trail, the last big snowflakes of March pirouetting around her, the dark trees awaiting her arrival.

She shouldn't have gone sledding alone at dusk. It would be hours before anyone found her, broken and bleeding, barely conscious. If they didn't find her before morning, she'd die from exposure.

At least it had been fun while it lasted—the wind sharp against her cheeks, her butt massaged by every bump, the shushing of millions of snowflakes beneath the sled, the melancholy twilight hush, this feeling of weightless timelessness.

She landed with a crunch.

Amid a tangle of dead branches, she waited for the pain to erupt from whatever she'd broken or sprained or punctured. When it failed to arrive, she knew she was paralyzed, her spine shattered—she'd spend the rest of her life in a wheelchair—and yet, she could feel her toes snug in her boots, her fingers in her mittens, her heart in her throat. She was sitting in the snow as if she'd meant to.

Euphoria bubbled up from her belly like sulphur dioxide from a mud pool, and she began to giggle. "Oh. my. God!" she screamed with relief, letting herself fall backward, arms spread wide, chest heaving with laughter. When at last she struggled to her feet, she had to wrestle the snow for ownership of her boots. She ran to retrieve the toboggan and continued downhill, on her stomach this time, the remaining slope almost sufficient to satisfy her desire for more.

She couldn't wait to tell Mom.

...

When Kyron awoke, it was to lurching rattles and absolute darkness. None of the myriad sounds or choking smells were familiar. He raised his wings to escape but lacked the space to stretch them full. No matter how he twisted or spun, his wings met something unyielding that thrummed and jangled. Panic overwhelmed him and he screamed, but his voice was swallowed by the growling darkness. He thrashed in every direction, bruising himself and bending feathers, increasing his violence with the single thought that if he gave it his all he would surely break free. When his beak caught against something thin and hard, he bit down on it, yanking his entire body back and forth until at last it gave way, and he pushed against it with the top of his head—only to find it no less solid. Baffled, he pushed harder, certain that he had felt the tendril snap. Not until he tried to bite down on it a second time did he understand it was his beak that had given way. He investigated the split with his tongue, and an abyssal sorrow engulfed him.

How long the darkness lasted he couldn't know, but in time it was pulled away, replaced by an orb as bright as lightning. Even after his eyes adjusted, the three figures looming behind it remained indistinct. One of them whistled like a songbird.

Kyron couldn't decide whether to spring at them, attempt to escape, or cringe in the corner of this gleaming, geometrical tangle, so he did none of these, but simply stood, squinting in the glare, trying to discern what sort of creatures they might be. One of the figures seemed to have the same reflective eyes as his captor. They chuckled like a murder of sleepy crows, then returned him to darkness with a thunderclap. He backed away as far as he could, hunched down, and focused all his will on refraining from further panic.

. . .

Mary Peabody was stirring soup when the back door opened, admitting Lissy, dripping snowmelt and wearing a triumphant grin.

"Shut the door, honey. It's cold out, okay? Where have you been?"

"Okay. So," Lissy said, carelessly slamming the door, "you know how you told me not to go sledding alone down Firetower Hill? Well. I hit this really big jump and just went flying into the woods. I thought. I was going. to die."

"Hang on a second," said Mary, holding out her hand like a crossing guard. "Are you telling me you went sledding, alone, down Firetower Hill, after I've told you how many times?"

"About a hundred. Anyway. I went flying into the woods, like–"

"Melissa Chrysanthemum Peabody, you are grounded."

"What? Mom, no!"

"No TV, no calling your friends, for a week."

"That's not fair! That's *so* not fair!"

"Why? How is that not fair? I've told you a thousand times–"

"Because I *told* you. Because. I could have just. not said anything, and you wouldn't. never have known, but you. I was *trusting* you, to just–"

"To what? To not get mad, when I've told you a million times not to go running off into the woods by yourself, and at night, no less? God knows what could have happened—you could get eaten by a bear—and who would save you? Not nobody, that's who. We've got a whole neighborhood here, kids your own age and everything. You could play with them for as long—until I called you in for dinner if you wanted to, but no."

"Oh my God, Mom, I'm not a little kid anymore. I'm thirteen years old. I don't 'play with the neighborhood kids' anymore, God."

She was sitting on the floor, pulling off her boots and wriggling out of her snow pants. She stood up, grabbed the tassel of her hat and flung it on her boots, her mouth pinched and white. She stalked out of the kitchen with the toes of her socks flapping.

Shaking her head, Mary returned to stirring the soup, much of which was now burned to the bottom of the pan.

* * *

Kyron was surrounded by angry ducks. He couldn't see them because the darkness was still absolute, but their quacking would wake a carcass. Was he dead, or had they eaten his eyes? He was lying on his side, on something as slick and unyielding as a wet rock. Every feather ached, and a keening moan escaped him. The ducks fell silent, but only for a moment.

As his mind grew clearer, he noticed his head was wrapped in something that was the source of his blindness. He noticed, too, that the calls he heard were too complex and varied for any waterfowl he knew. He had to assume he was in the company of humans.

Strangely, the realization brought a certain measure of calm. If humans were responsible for his blindness, then terror was what they desired from him. He would not oblige. His body still felt waterlogged and disconnected, but he was not yet dead, and so long as he lived there was the possibility of escape.

He touched his tongue to the part of his beak that had broken. The tear had closed, but it tasted sharp and bitter, like rotted fish. He clenched his jaw and felt a twinge that pulled at something deep within his breast. The damage was not yet healed, but the something deep inside was strong. Drawing upon that strength, he tried to heave himself upright. It took several attempts, during which he batted his head several times against the hard surface beneath him—producing a hollow boom that echoed oddly in his mind—but in the end he managed it.

Once upright, it took all his resolve to stay that way. He was weak but not yet defeated. Blind though he was, he took several deep breaths in preparation for flight, but before he could raise his wings, rough talons grasped him around the middle and he was lifted. Once again, a sense of helplessness overwhelmed him and fear battled his resolve, but he was quickly released and his head uncovered, revealing a row of orbs, each as bright as any sun. He blinked and shook his head, trying to clear the spots that floated before him no matter which direction he looked. He was dimly aware of a human form backing away from him, and of a host of human faces staring from behind the suns.

Abruptly, they fell silent, as if waiting for him to act. He opened his beak, but a strangely rounded human approached from one side and squawked at the flock of faces with all the undignified indignation of a goose, waving its malformed wings ineffectually. When the human was done honking, it waddled back the way it had come. Immediately it returned and repeated the performance. It did this several times, until Kyron began to wonder if he were dreaming.

The sense of unreality overpowered the threat he perceived from the humans, and he risked a look behind. To his horror he found himself surrounded by gigantic insects similar to the one that had attacked his aerie. Lined up in eerily ordered rows, they stood sinister and motionless. Even worse, he was standing on the face of one. His talons were scratching the same hard surface he had met when he slammed into the monster's underbelly, and suddenly he recalled where he had heard that hollow boom before.

He tried to scream and leap away, but his aching body would not obey. Instead he only squawked and fell over. Immediately he started sliding horribly down to where the creature's mouth must be. When a human scooped him off the monster's face, he was almost grateful, even as another human slipped something over his head that returned his blindness. For the moment, those rough talons felt as safe as his mother's, and he only prayed that they would bear him far away and never let him go.

3.

Kyron awoke to stars and a fragrant breeze. His head was throbbing painfully, but there was a lump of unidentifiable flesh beside him, which he ate with only the slightest hesitation. It was surprisingly soft and reasonably fresh. With his hunger assuaged, the pain receded, and he gradually grew aware that he was not alone. The cries of a host of other animals arose from every direction. Mournful cries, mostly—the huff of a bear, the hoot of an owl, the yip of a coyote, the squabble of a fox—these he recognized, but other sounds were as foreign to him as the meat. The whole place felt forsaken and unreal, and the darkness, punctured by sickly yellow moons, felt eternal. Turning his back on the lights and sounds, he stared at the dim cliff face behind him and searched his heart for the tell-tale tug that indicated the direction back to Corwynn: the direction in which he would fly as soon as morning arrived—assuming it ever did.

4.

The rising sun turned the cliff before him as blue and white as any sky should be, if unnaturally still and flat. Beneath the sky-cliff was a leafless green forest, motionless and somehow too close. Looking at it made his eyes hurt. Above him was a giant spider's web, blocking the way to a deeper, brighter sky. A second and third web extended on either side from the web above to the ground below. In a flash of panic-inducing intuition, he jumped and spun. Indeed: a fourth web confirmed his suspicion that he was caught in a larger version of the jangling tangle that had brought him here—a place designed to cut him off from Corwynn.

The tree branch upon which he perched was as hard as a rock. It was crenelated like bark, and stretched outward from a trunk, but there was no give to it. No matter how hard he gripped, his talons made no impression.

To keep his mounting panic at bay, he preened, running his beak through feathers unaccountably still warm and pliable. How long till he became as rigid and unyielding as branch and sky?

Spring

5.

Mary licked the envelope on the last of the bills and pushed back from the table with a sigh. It was well after midnight, and the hum of the wall clock set off a ringing in her ears. She should have gone to bed hours ago, and, thinking how tired she would be at work tomorrow, she considered calling in sick, except that she'd have to get up early anyway to see Lissy off to school. She ran her fingers through her hair and forced herself to stand up.

Hoping to find solace in the sight of her sleeping child, she opened the door to Lissy's room. Unfortunately, as her eyes adjusted to the darkness, the only things visible were clothes and schoolbooks and papers strewn haphazardly across the floor. All she could discern of her daughter was a lump in the bed, and all she felt was growing annoyance at the mess.

"Mom?" said a sleepy voice. "What's wrong?"

"Good night, Lissy," Mary said.

"Good night," said Lissy in that horrible teenage voice she had developed that ridiculed her mother's every gesture.

"Sleep tight, honey."

"I was."

Mary shut the door and stalked down the hall to her room. She could remember using the same voice toward her own parents when she was thirteen, but the memory brought little comfort. She was angry and tired, and the combination gave her a headache. She stretched herself onto the bed without taking off her clothes and forced herself to sleep.

Failing that, she got up, grabbed a jacket and went outside for a walk.

She set off at a brisk pace. It was chilly, and the jacket wasn't nearly warm enough, but her mind was distracted by too many thoughts to pay much attention to temperature.

"I need a break, Lord," she said. "I can't keep doing this. I can't keep doing it alone. I *can't*, Lord. Please."

Twenty minutes later, she was walking off the end of the sidewalk and traipsing through the edge of somebody's field. The dead and frosted grass crunched beneath her feet.

She wished Michael's parents lived nearby; they would be happy to take Lissy in for a few weeks, and Lissy probably wouldn't mind staying with them, but there was no money for airfare, and she didn't want to send her daughter that far away. She felt guilty for wanting to send her away at all, but the feeling that her life was not her own was overwhelming. It had been almost three years since Michael walked out on them, and Mary still had not regained her sense of self. She needed time alone for that, and too much of her focus had been spent worrying that Lissy would take Michael's desertion personally.

Lissy hadn't spent much time with her other grandparent, Mary's own father, since her mother passed away a year and a half ago. He was a guarded, silent man, and Lissy had always been a little afraid of him. She would probably resist the idea of staying with him for any amount of time, but on the other hand he would probably love the company. Whether he would say it out loud or not was another question, but that big old house must be lonely for him, and he was only forty-five minutes away. . . .

She stopped, lips pursed. It was not a perfect solution, but it was a solution, or at least the idea of one. Honestly, it felt like an answer to her prayer.

She turned, twisting grass beneath one foot, and walked back home. She didn't remember much of the return journey, preoccupied as she was with nurturing a tender seedling of hope.

...

"I could just fucking leave," he muttered. It was four in the morning, and Calvin Berman was sitting on the edge of his bed, one hand inside a bag of corn chips. He'd been up for two hours contemplating the proposition that life was a meaningless string of random occurrences and therefore he could do whatever he wanted and it wouldn't matter. His brother Shawn had been on the topic for days, and, although Calvin rarely paid attention to the meaningless string of random words that spooled from his brother's lips, he had found himself strangely excited. Even now, he was leaning forward, shifting his weight off the bed and onto his toes, chewing once every three or four seconds. Abruptly, he stood, his knees crackling.

He glanced out the window, where faintly he could make out the silhouette of trees against the sky, then scanned his room, noticing the backpack, the hunting knife, the bow and arrows, his camouflage pants and shirt draped over a chair. It wasn't much, but it would let him survive for awhile in the woods until he found somewhere . . . anywhere away from this house, this town, this father. He would miss the last month or so of his junior year of high school, but not very much.

"I could actually fucking leave."

As the reality of the idea grew within him, it sank into his belly and touched off a feeling of elation so powerful that he sat back down to contemplate it, only to find it dissipate as quickly as it had erupted.

It was always like that: his emotions had no staying power in his brain. It had been that way even when his mother died: Whenever tears had begun to rise, a part of him had stepped back, like a butterfly collector nearly treading upon a rare specimen, fumbling with his net to capture it before it flew away but never being quick enough, and always ending up feeling empty and depressed, until it seemed depression was the only emotion he could sustain.

Depression, to that detached entomologist in his brain, was about as interesting as a housefly. Impressive in its own way, perhaps, but after watching it bounce off the same pane of glass for days on end, he just wanted it to hurry up and die.

He was convinced that emotions were the key to his personality. If only he could feel something too huge to fade away, perhaps he would meet his true self, the man who was hiding in his skin. His mother's death didn't qualify only because he didn't like to think about it. Perhaps running away from home would be enormous enough without overloading his circuits, but today was not the day for that—today he was too depressed.

Besides, there were still patches of snow in the woods, even though it was April. Surviving in the wild would be easier once edible plants started growing and edible creatures ventured from their holes to eat them.

• • •

Corwynn scratched at the body of the pregnant rabbit she'd killed. Two of her own children had poked an egg tooth through their shells, their peeps lending fresh urgency to the hunt—to the need to build up strength even in the dim light before dawn—but filling her also with remorse at the death of another mother. She couldn't bear to think of eating the naked, pink bodies squirming in their mother's brown and blood-soaked fur.

Kyron would have eaten them. He would have honored the cruelty of their deaths by granting a merciful end to their hopeless lives. But she was not Kyron—she was shame incarnate. She walked away, several awkward paces, then jumped heavily into the air, flying low over the meadow. The thought of the dead mother dragged at her flight, making her heart too heavy for the wind. She wasn't going to clear the top of the approaching tree, so she grabbed it, rooting herself precipitously. Not even a branch could uphold her mass without a struggle, but Corwynn clenched the green wood as if to crush it, until at last it stopped swaying.

She wanted to swallow herself whole, to dig out the gnawing pain in her chest with her beak, but she was helpless, frozen. She couldn't fly away from the uneaten, pregnant rabbit, nor could she return to it.

She glared at the mountain, home to her unprotected eggs. They were raccoon food; best to let them go. It would be impossible to take care of them by herself once they hatched. Maybe one, but not all three. She should choose one and push the other two out of the nest.

In her mind she saw two smashed eggs at the base of the tree, but the imagined bodies spilling out of the shells were pink rabbit pups.

Panic overwhelmed her like a cloudburst. The world was too big. There was sky in every direction and no Kyron anywhere. She squeezed her eyes shut, as if blindness could change anything. The panic flowed in past every feather, soaking her skin, and there was nothing she could do to abate the flood.

From a small knot in the center of her breast rose an image of healthy hatchlings, hungry and vulnerable, which was followed immediately by a fierce desire to protect and feed them. Like summer sun, the bright image drew the damp panic from her feathers and replaced the impossibility of the task with the certainty that never again would she flee any danger that imperiled them.

She searched her inmost being for any contradiction, but there was none. Her own life meant nothing to her; she was free to give it as Kyron had given his.

She let go of the tree.

The wind caught her.

. . .

Kyron had never had much interest in humans, but now they filled his mind from his startled awakening at dawn, alert for the sound of thunder, to his slipping into fitful dozing, disturbed by dreams of growling darkness. Before his capture, humans had been smallish figures of varying colors far below him. Occasionally, he had seen them congregating in a field, like geese pausing from their winter migration, but he had thought them generally to be solitary creatures, walking or gliding alongside the black hunting trails of gigantic gleaming beetles, or wandering outside their elaborately enclosed nests. Only rarely had he glimpsed any crawling the side of his mountain on their long hind legs.

Here humans wandered freely on the other side of the thick, unsticky spider web, occasionally stopping to gaze at him unafraid. At first, he had fled from them—especially the ones with shiny, reflective eyes—but there was nowhere to go, and they made no move to attack, so he had learned to suffer their stares with a modicum of dignity, and in time he began to notice some surprising details.

They all, without exception, appeared to be in advanced stages of molting. Their faces, particularly around the eyes, were bare and smooth, but their breasts and limbs were of various colors—often multicolored—and their plumage was so droopy Kyron couldn't figure out how it was still attached. The tops of their heads likewise varied in length and color, and appeared to be fur grown as long as tail feathers. In some cases longer. Even here, though, the occasional human would be deplumed on top. The plump, wormlike appendages on the ends of their flat paws turned out to be more nimble than any raccoon's, and they clutched many things, from each other's paws to objects that defied categorization.

He couldn't tell the difference between the males and females but assumed that the larger ones with furrier faces were probably female. Some had sacks or pouches hanging at their sides or on their backs. Their calls were muted, for the most part, though some of them chittered like squirrels, but he could sense no pattern in their vocalizations—it was as if they didn't mean anything, or perhaps they were always hungry. Many of them were eating even as they stared at him, though he recognized no living things among their food.

Strangest of all, groups of two or more would often turn their backs to him and huddle close while one of their number stood a few paces off and held up one of their inexplicable objects. Every time this happened, Kyron was reminded unpleasantly of blinding lights, a squawking human, and shiny rows of beetle monsters.

***

Mary was startled from sleep by a man's voice squawking at her to "buy the car of your dreams!" She slapped the alarm clock and he shut up. "Oh God," she moaned. "Oh, God." She swung her legs out of bed and heaved herself into a sitting position. Her head was ringing.

Why on earth had she taken a walk at two o'clock in the morning? She was going to be useless at work. She struggled with the desire to sway gently back onto the mattress, then forced herself to stand. Absently, she turned the alarm function off so it wouldn't start squawking again, then headed for the shower.

The water hit her chest like a draft of hot cocoa. *What did people do before there were showers?* she wondered.

Not work in offices, she answered. *They just splashed cold water on their faces and stumbled into the fields to dig turnips without worrying about how they smelled.* Digging turnips sounded like a pleasant change—milking cows, churning butter—whatever it was they did before hot showers became a necessity. She thought of farms and searched her mind for what else they reminded her of. *Fatty foods? No.* She was probably trying to remember a dream, but she didn't have the patience to concentrate. She turned off the water and reached for her towel. She had to make sure Lissy was up and getting ready for school.

Lissy. Farms. Aha! She had been thinking of sending Lissy to Dad's house for a few weeks. It was the sort of thought that sounded good late at night but was utterly unworkable once the sun rose. Lissy would hate it out there in the middle of nowhere with nothing to do and no one to do it with but an old man who rarely even spoke. Besides, she didn't *want* Lissy to go away this summer. Sure, it seemed overwhelming at times to raise a teenage daughter all alone, but she could handle it. A few late-night panic attacks were a small price to pay for the pleasure of having a daughter to hang around with all summer. They'd have fun. She returned the towel to its rack and stepped out of the shower.

When she walked into the kitchen, Lissy was at the table, mechanically eating cereal, staring dully at the box and slurping loudly.

"Morning, Sunshine," said Mary, conscious that her cheery voice must grate on her daughter's nerves. Lissy didn't even grunt in reply. For a moment, Mary considered asking her if she'd like to spend a few weeks with Grandpa, but immediately thought better of it. For one thing, she hadn't even asked Dad, and for another, she couldn't really imagine telling her daughter she needed a break from her. She pulled a bowl and a spoon from the dishwasher and set them on the table.

When she picked up the cereal box, Lissy glared at her. Evidently she had been reading it. Mary poured her cereal and placed the box precisely back where it had been. Lissy shifted it a quarter of an inch and continued reading. While Mary poured milk, Lissy stood up, tossed her bowl in the sink with a clatter, then plodded heavily upstairs to her room.

"Don't go back to sleep, honey; the bus will be here in fifteen minutes."

"I know, Mom."

Mary couldn't explain, even to herself, why Lissy's tone was hurtful. It hadn't been so long ago that she'd been in the habit of doing just that—going back to sleep instead of getting ready—but now she acted as if no fool in the known universe would do such a profoundly stupid thing, and her mother might as well remind her not to eat nails. Mary smiled, remembering when Lissy had been two or three and gotten into a box of framing brads. How she had cried when Mary had screamed at her to spit them out.

Mary finished her cereal, cleared the table and got out her Bible and devotional. The bookmarks opened to Genesis 22. She read the chapter heading and closed the book abruptly. "The Command to Sacrifice Isaac" was not the story she needed prayerfully to be considering right now. She left the table and finished getting ready for work.

6.

Corwynn raised her wings and opened her mouth—the same stance Kyron had adopted when the dragon attacked—but she meant it differently, her hiss not a warning but a plea; her third egg was several days past due. With infinitely gentle care she stretched her mouth over the egg, so that the tips of her beak touched its top and bottom and her tongue pressed against its side. Again she hissed, softly, eyes closed, willing her breath to pass through the shell. Three times she breathed on it before she withdrew and opened her eyes.

Her other chicks were peeping, hungry and insistent, but she had no difficulty ignoring them.

She heard a tap. It might have been the wind tapping two nearby twigs together, but her maternal ear knew better. She rested her cheek against the shell and listened so intently that the rest of the world folded up and disappeared. Another tap, and she had located her tardy eaglet's beak.

Keenly aware of the danger, she rapped the tip of her own beak smartly against that single point. The egg remained unbroken, so she tapped again, more sharply. By now, her breathing had grown rapid.

Switching tactics, she placed one foot upon the recalcitrant shell. Positioning her back talon precisely where her chick's beak must be, she began, with unearthly patience, to squeeze. Her heart was close to breaking for fear of crushing the tiny life inside, and her jaw was clenched in concentration. Her standing leg began to cramp, but her rear talon was sharp, and with it she opened a tiny hole. She stepped back, breathless. Within moments a tiny egg tooth filled the gap. A tiny peep promised to keep tapping from the inside out.

Corwynn turned and pulled a piece of flesh from the dead squirrel beside her to feed her other eaglets.

7.

CORWYNN DANGLED THE STRIP OF FISH WHERE NONE BUT HER YOUNGEST could reach. He was so weak he could barely support his own head, while his brother and sister were quick to snatch every morsel. It worried her, especially when she was hunting. She might return to find him pecked to death or pushed from the nest. She did her best to provide plenty for everyone, but hunting was long work, and with each passing dawn her exhaustion deepened. The world grew oddly colored, apt to sway in alarming directions. The best times were at night, when her only responsibility was to keep watch. She dozed in fragments, but jolted away from any deeper sleep. She imagined herself as an egg, hard and durable, enclosing three eaglets. The days might blur, but night always came eventually.

At length her youngest found the fish, swallowed, continued to live.

8.

Corwynn returned to the nest with a raccoon that was far too big. It had taken three tries to reach the nest, and each time she rose she caught another glimpse of her daughter pushing and pecking at her youngest son.

By the time she finally lugged the raccoon into the aerie, her son looked dazed, and she was surprised to find she recognized his expression. Her two eldest were peeping lustily, eager for meat, but Corwynn was lost in a memory that had the quality of a dream.

The aerie of her own fledglinghood: She rarely thought of it except when she was expanding her own, wondering how she could ever make hers as big. She had been middle-hatched—in awe of her big sister and resentful of her little brother. How often had she seen that same dazed look in his eyes? Whenever there was food to be had, she would peck at him to let him know that she and her sister would eat first. When her parents were gone, she'd push him toward the edge of the nest. Her parents would nudge him back toward the middle, but never made any other move to stop her. As she grew stronger, her pecks had begun to draw blood, until at last he had fallen over and ceased trying to rise.

How proud and strong she had felt in that moment! Her father, standing beside them the whole time, had lifted the limp body with his beak and tossed it out of the aerie. At last, it was just her and her big sister, sharing everything until they learned to fly.

The peeping of her eldest chicks grew louder, but her son's swimming eyes consumed her. She watched him gather for his own feeble peep, but his sister leaned over and pecked him on the top of his head. Without thinking, Corwynn did the same to her—a sharp peck that drew a small drop of blood. Her daughter shook her head and looked around, as though unclear from whence the pain had come. At last her eyes found her mother's, and she cocked her head in surprise. "Peep!" she cried.

Corwynn's heart was racing as she turned her attention back to the raccoon and began to take it apart. This time, she made sure the biggest pieces went to her daughter, who yanked them from her beak and dropped them, preferring to eat from the ground rather than accept her mother's guilt offerings.

Each time it happened pierced Corwynn's heart, but she hardened her will should a second lesson be required.

Summer, Part 1

9.

Something in the way the freshly-tilled soil yielded to Ed Nowlen's feet, while at the same time supporting his weight, reminded him of Karen, and consoled him now that she was gone. He closed his eyes and breathed the warm, spring air—he could almost take off his shoes.

Imagining it was enough—he knew the feel of dirt between his toes and knew, too, that it would be colder than he'd wish, and how the grit would feel in his socks afterwards, causing blisters. He was too rickety, anyhow, to reach all the way down to untie his laces. The rototiller's thrum was still in his arms and chest; it had worn him out more than he cared to admit.

"We're getting old, Shep," he said to the dog who lay in the grass, enjoying the sun and thumping his tail in response to his name. Shep was a Golden Retriever/St. Bernard mix who was older, in dog years, than Ed. His fur was clumping and he suffered from arthritis, but his bearing was no less regal. Ed reached into his pocket for a dog biscuit and tossed it underhand, bouncing it off the dog's nose. Shep jerked his head away, then sneezed. For a moment, their eyes met, and Ed wondered how to interpret the empty gaze. Was it reproach? Shame? Scorn? A warning that he'd better not laugh? Or was it simply the eternal, inexplicable sorrow of dogs?

"What's the matter? That was a good throw."

Without shifting his weight, Shep twisted his neck and snatched up the biscuit. After the first bite, he dropped the pieces back in the grass, so he could eat them one at a time.

Ed turned his gaze to the field. The hay was half-grown, a green he had loved since childhood. A few gulls floated over it, a few swooping sparrows, but he saw no sign of woodchuck or rabbit. He checked the sky and surrounding trees, but there were only a couple of crows bobbing in the tiptop pine boughs. Not so much as an airplane marred the pristine blue.

It was time to get back to work, but his body was complaining, and, although he didn't often pay attention to it, his heart was keening. Hoping to outpace it, he strode to the apple tree where he'd left his walking stick, and whistled for Shep to join him.

He skirted the edge of the field—not wanting to trample the hay—and headed for the gate in the corner. Walking along the old stone wall, he noticed that it was getting overgrown; he'd need to come through with the brush cutter one of these days.

Halfway to the gate, he stopped to wipe sweat from the corners of his eyes with his sleeve. Mid-eighties the weatherman had predicted, but tonight it would rain again and cool down.

He pulled the gate open and waited for Shep to trundle through. From long habit, he turned and looked back at the house. It was a modest, two-story, clapboard building with two chimneys. Not much to look at, some might say, but beyond it was the mountain, rising half a mile to the south and seeming to shelter his home in its enormous wings. Again he thought of Karen.

For forty years she had stood beside him here at the end of their evening walks, enjoying this same wide view. He sagged against his walking stick. The whistling lament of his heart was so high-pitched only Shep could have heard it, were it an actual sound. "Lord," he said, his voice breaking. "Lord Almighty."

He stared at the hard-packed sand at his feet, searching his mind for words to express what his heart was howling. "I know I should be grateful for those forty years, but . . . I never expected. I never wanted to . . ." he watched a tear shatter in the road, creating a tiny crater in the dust.

He wiped his nose with his sweat-soaked sleeve and, with a ragged breath, pulled a cigarette out and lit it. After the first puff the tears receded. He straightened up, turned his back on the mountain, and followed the road into the trees.

* * *

The ache in Shep's hips made him long to stop walking. The comforting smells of trees and dirt and the delicious aroma of chipmunk and squirrel were tainted by the acrid, metallic taste of pain. It had not always been thus. Once upon a time, Shep had greeted any hint that Good might take him on a Walk with a joy like summer rain: violent and refreshing. The memory of that joy still visited him, but, each time, the pain became all but unbearable a little more quickly. To make things worse, sand worked into the spaces between his pads, making them tender. He knew from experience that stopping to lick his feet now would only make the rest of the Walk feel worse, so he gathered the pains to his chest and held them as best he could.

* * *

Æthel, from the dim enclosure of her hollow tree, could hear the chatter of seven different kinds of birds, as well as various and assorted fur-bearing animals, frogs, and insects. Some days it was difficult to get any sleep at all.

More unbearable than the noise, however, was her longing to join their frolics. Normally, her only contact with other animals came when she swooped down upon them in the night, carried them back to her tree and ate them, but she was more than a mere predator; just once she would like to demonstrate that she, too, was a child of the pristine air, with the same longings, the same joys and sorrows as they.

She poked her head out and looked around. The sun sent sparkling green fire glancing through pine needles, producing colors Æthel rarely saw. Her heart leaped within her, like a nestling just discovering she can fly. Without pausing to consider—hooting with exhilaration—she swooped from the tree.

At first, she mistook the screams of jays as answering calls of joy and welcome, but other birds fell silent, the squirrels scolded, and a small army of sparrows mobbed her in a decidedly unwelcoming fashion. They flapped about her, their tiny beaks twisting away tufts of feathers, battering her from every direction. No matter how she rolled and swooped or flapped and dodged, they maintained their attack until she began to doubt her survival. At last, miraculously, she regained her tree and huddled, shaking in the dimness, waiting for her assailants to follow her into her home.

Instead, after a bit, the jays stopped screaming and the seven other kinds of birds resumed their song. It was as if she had never interrupted them. As if she had ceased to exist.

When, finally, she slipped into a troubled sleep, she dreamed herself disintegrating: feathers, talons, and beak falling away as she flew through sunlit trees.

．．．

Shep stopped and pricked up his ears. His hearing had muted somewhat with age, but he thought he had heard an owl call out a raucous greeting. His tail wagged in response, though he knew the greeting could not have been directed at him. Perhaps the owl's mate had returned after a long absence.

Shep looked at Good, who was limping along, taking no notice of the uproar in the forest. Shep cocked his head to one side. In one of those rare flashes of insight that visited him from time to time, he saw how old his pack leader was, how full of sorrow and even loneliness. Suddenly they all seemed connected: the owl, the dog, and the man. The owl was now hooting unhappily—pain mixed with despair. Whatever had prompted her initial outburst had evidently not been what she'd hoped. Shep could sympathize. No one ever seemed to greet him with the same eagerness with which he greeted them. With fondness, yes, but rarely with joy.

The one exception used to be Pumpkin, Good's whelp. When Shep had first joined the pack, Pumpkin had squealed with delight to see him and had showered him with affection for days on end. In time, her enthusiasm waned, but by then Shep already had fallen in love. He had hoped one day they would mate, but she had left the pack when he still was young, and returned only occasionally with a mate who stood on two legs—one of her own kind—and soon they had a whelp of their own. A deep part of Shep still felt an aching chasm where his hopes for their impossible union once had dwelt. He had never taken a mate nor sired a litter, and now he likely never would. The thought merely added to the pains of the day.

Good turned and slapped his leg, summoning him. Shep lurched into motion, his hips going white for a moment with pain. When he caught up, Good claimed him as his own, saying, "Good dog," and reached down to scratch him under one ear.

It was a little, common gesture, but it set Shep in his place. Good had lost his mate and his whelp. He too was old and footsore. They were down to a pack of two, and all they had was each other. Shep pondered this final insight for the remainder of the Walk, and he found that his pain diminished in proportion to the attention he focused on Good. By the time they reached the house, he was filled with affection for this human who faithfully provided him with food and comfort.

He bounded up the steps to the door, regretting only that he had not spent more time thinking about his friend. When Good let him in, he trotted to his water dish to slake his thirst then curled up beside the stove and began earnestly to lick his feet.

"Poor old pup," said Good, on his way to the Fridge. Shep slapped his tail against the floor. He *felt* like a pup. An exceedingly wise and happy pup. He closed his eyes and swallowed, scouring the joy and sorrow lodged in his throat with the blood and grit from his feet.

10.

Calvin stood by the window with his backpack on his shoulders, bow and quiver in one hand, with the other flat against the glass. In the weeks since the idea of running away had occurred, he had managed to procure some food and even a little bit of money. "No more excuses," he told himself, sternly.

His heart was beating heavily, like someone rhythmically pounding a nail, and his hand began to slide down the glass on a film of sweat. A sudden image of his father walking in caused his heart to take one more hammer then stop.

He should unpack, put everything away exactly as it had been before, and go back to sleep.

Instead, his hand reached for the clasp, which turned easily. All he needed to do was lift the window and step outside.

He listened intently for sounds from the hall, but there was only Shawn's alarm clock, a beeping that would continue for at least another hour. With a deep breath and an unintended prayer, he raised first the window, then the screen, and lifted one leg onto the sill.

For a moment his strength faltered, until something electric flashed through him. *Was that anger?* He shoved the leg roughly outside. It was an awkward squeeze, especially when he hung for a second with his stomach on the sill before dropping almost a foot, leaving a swath of fire on his torso. Leaning against the house and cradling his belly, he drew in a "Ssssssssss!" through his teeth.

He reached up and pulled the window down, decided not to bother with the screen, then fled, crouched down like a thief.

At the edge of the back yard, the ground sloped down to the river, and he ran full out, dodging trees and leaping over rocks, exhilarated by his own agility. The dimmer light beneath the trees lent a dreamlike quality to his descent, almost as if he were in a movie. Faster and faster he pushed himself, letting gravity add to his momentum, twisting around brakes and boles like an action hero chased by double agents. Once, when a boulder loomed too quickly, he dove over it and rolled, twisting his backpack and jabbing his cheek with the tip of his bow before leaping back up in one fluid motion and running on.

When he reached the edge of the river, he bent over, gasping hoarsely, his whole body trembling but his heart filled with something that was surely joy. He wished he had the nerve to go back and do it again. He shrugged off his pack and the bow and quiver, and forced himself to walk haltingly back and forth along the bank, stretching his muscles to keep them from cramping.

Once his breathing steadied, he sat down on a rock to figure out his next move. He had at least an hour before anyone noticed he was missing. He envisioned his father and brother coming after him, using their German Shepherd, Butchy, to track him through the woods. Butchy would find him, too: Calvin was the only one of them the dog actually liked. Horrified regret swelled like an ocean wave in his chest and up into his throat. How could he have left Butchy behind? Dad hated the dog, and Shawn was indifferent. Instead of running *from* him, he could be running *with* him. Why hadn't he thought of that? But going back now was out of the question.

Belatedly, he realized he was feeling something intense, so he focused on the panic, but as quickly as it had come, it was gone.

The proposed meaninglessness of the universe presumably meant it didn't matter that he'd left his dog behind, or whether Butchy found him. Neither did it matter that his mother was dead, or that he couldn't seem to get too worked up about it. If he fell in the river and drowned, it wouldn't matter. If he went back home and lived with Dad until they ended up killing each other, that wouldn't matter, either. He was utterly free, free to choose from 360 different directions—any point on the compass.

He looked around: Mist was curling up from the river's surface; the trees were gaining definition in the growing light; his house, at the top of the slope, sat like a cow anticipating rain.

He took a deep breath. The ragged edges of his earlier panic shuddered through his lungs but once again subsided, replaced this time with a fierce longing for the one direction denied him. As ridiculous as it seemed, what he wanted more than anything was to shuck gravity and leap into the air.

It occurred to him that he could try: He had already done one impossible thing this morning, why not another?

The idea made him blush. He could picture himself rocketing skyward, leaving depression and indecision behind, the little house by the river dwindling into an insignificant speck, but he could also picture the group of kids hiding behind a clump of trees, ready to laugh at his pathetic attempt at a mighty hop.

"I think I'll try upriver," he said, mostly for the benefit of the hidden, hypothetical children.

His pack, when he put it on, felt cold on his overheated back. He couldn't find a comfortable angle for his bow, but he decided it didn't matter; he took a deep breath and stepped into the river.

It was less than knee deep but shockingly cold. For a minute he simply stood there, legs atremble, lungs gasping, heart straining to pump blood up and away from his feet, until the pain—that somehow reached all the way up to his ears—finally receded somewhat and he could feel the push of the current against his shins. He took an unsteady step forward.

It was stupid, of course: The alternative to the theory that life was meaningless was that it was not, in which case he was stupid not to know that and doubly stupid to be wading upriver in the growing light of dawn, hoping to throw his pet German Shepherd off his scent. By tomorrow he would almost certainly be glad to be found.

"Well, so I'm stupid," he muttered, though he couldn't hear himself over the babbling water. "If anything means anything, then that must mean something, too."

. . .

For Lissy, sitting on the bleachers with her friends on the last day of eighth grade, the scene was tinged with an odd nostalgia, as if she were ninety years old, looking back on her long-ago childhood. The four of them: herself, Jenna, Heather, and Beth Anne, had been best friends since fifth grade, ever since the three girls had gathered around after her Dad left, laying hands on her and murmuring indistinct words of comfort that sent rushes of feeling cascading through a body that moments before had been numb. They were not the most popular girls, nor even the nicest, but they had stood beside her when no one else had, and she felt a certain obligation to them, so that, even when she wished she could spend recess with someone else, she always stuck by them. Over time, obligation had given way to devotion.

Today, Jenna was prattling about how they would all be best friends forever, throughout high school and beyond—in years to come they would all live next door to each other and stand around talking just like this while their children cavorted around them. It made Lissy angry, because it was a lie: this was the end. After tonight's graduation ceremony, they would drift apart, make other friends, and after high school they'd move away, scattering to the four winds.

Lissy wanted to remember every detail of this last afternoon, from the feel of the metal bleachers to the gigantic puddle in the middle of left field to the sounds of yells and traffic that surrounded them. Most of all she wanted to remember her three friends.

"Stop spacing out, Lissy, God," said Jenna. "I asked you a question."

Lissy turned her attention from the way the sunlight seemed caught in Beth Anne's hair and looked at Jenna. "Huh?"

They laughed indulgently, all except Beth Anne, who said meekly, "Jenna was asking who you wanted to marry."

"Oh. I don't know. God. No one from here."

"Lissy's going to marry someone from Italy," said Heather, "who's moved here to work in his uncle's restaurant. They're going to have twelve children and live in Beth Anne's garage." Lissy laughed; Heather's tone was always mocking, but her jabs were so imaginative they rarely had much bite.

"No," said Jenna, who could always turn Heather's jokes into something mean. "She's going to marry someone from Mexico, who moved here to mow people's lawns. They're going to live in . . ." She did have trouble finishing her stories, though.

Beth Anne said, "I think that . . ."

"A dumpster," said Jenna.

Beth Anne looked down. There was a slight pause.

"Come *on*," said Jenna. "Just pick someone. It's not like we're going to hold you to it."

"Fine. Timmy Capps." ("Ewww!" said all three at once) "I'm going to marry Timmy Capps, we're going to have three-and-a-half kids and live in your nostril."

"You're weird," said Jenna, but Heather was grinning, and Beth Anne's lips were primly trying not to smile, so Lissy didn't mind Jenna's sneer.

The bell rang, and Lissy's smile faltered. Suddenly she wanted to hug all three of them and cry together over the end of their childhood, but the three were already running toward the door. Glumly, Lissy took one last look around—at the baseball diamond and the trees and the clouds, trying to sear it all into her memory—then turned and followed them in.

* * *

Calvin could get through most days without thinking about his mother, but not today. He was walking down a muddy track that must once have been a logging road. He was hungry and anxious about his ability to gather food, but he could shove those things to the periphery of his awareness. The string of his bow was digging into his shoulder, he had a blister on one heel and a dire need to relieve his bladder, but he could ignore all that. His mother, though, was nagging him as surely as if she were walking beside him, fresh from the grave.

"You're like your father, only better," she used to say. "Where were you when I was looking for a husband?" The question had always unnerved him. He could understand why, now, but at the time he had half-thought she was serious. He had wondered if Dad would be jealous if he found out, and whether she really expected her son to take the hint and move her out of there.

His legs were aching. He had been walking since before dawn, and it was now close to noon. He looked for a place he could step off the track, take a leak, and comfortably sit a spell, but the undergrowth was uniformly tangled and the ground boggy on both sides. As he continued, a strange panic rose up within him. He was light-headed, and there was no place to turn aside and rest. Crazily, he thought of Mary and Joseph in Bethlehem, looking for an inn.

He forced his legs to walk faster, jumping stiff-legged over rivulets and passing up half-decent rest spots with the thought that there would be something better around the next bend. It didn't make any sense, but he couldn't stop—he needed to find the perfect place that he knew was just a little bit farther ahead.

At last he could go no further—his bladder was ready to burst—so he unzipped his fly and relieved himself into the mud at his feet, intensely aware of the hikers, Fish and Game wardens, and Girl Scout Troops that would walk into view at any moment. Once his bladder was empty, the panic receded. He buttoned his fly, sidestepped his puddle, and walked on. Not ten minutes later, he reached a large, flat rock, sunwarmed and dry: the place ordained. There was even a gap in the underbrush about the size of a urinal. His bladder still ached from the strain he had put on it, but part of him wished he had held out just a little while longer.

⋄ ⋄ ⋄

Kyron had long since lost interest in his visitors, but when the littlest of three humans stretched its foreleg through the web as though proffering the chubby little talons on the end of it, he was tempted to fly over and nip one off. One of its parents pulled it away, and, while Kyron was pleased by this rare display of respect for the danger he posed, the protective gesture reminded him keenly of Corwynn and his eggs.

Suddenly, he wanted the humans gone. They were standing too close together, their limbs wrapped around each other, a stark reminder of what he had lost, what had been taken from him. He shook his head convulsively, trying to contain the surge of despair and panic in his breast, while the three just stood there, gaping. The biggest one hid its face behind one of those ubiquitous rock-like things that weren't rocks. When part of the object exploded with light, Kyron found himself attacking, launching his beak and talons at the three of them, striking the thick webbing with a clang. All three of the humans leaped backward, and the smallest began to wail. Again, he threw himself at them and again was rebuffed. A third time and he was clinging to the webbing, his head thrust through a gap, his beak snapping, and at last the parents led their screaming offspring away.

Strangely, their leaving caused an even greater pang in his heart, and he called out to them to return. The tall one looked back—for a moment their eyes locked—and then they were gone.

That night, as he huddled on the ground, helpless and defeated, ignoring the meal dropped beside him, the eyes of the human parent lingered still. All night long, in the midst of his despair, those eyes seemed to watch over him, until eventually he fell asleep.

11.

In the eerie glow cast by low, heavy clouds, Æthel sat perched on a branch, swaying in tight circles. She was having trouble keeping both eyes open at the same time—as soon as she opened one the other began to droop. She tried to focus on sounds, listening for the scritch of prey, but she hadn't been able to sleep since the ruckus she'd caused, and she couldn't stop flinching every time a moth swooped past her. Sometimes there was no moth, just the ghost of a midday sparrow attacking her shoulder.

She twisted her head fully around, once in each direction, stretching the muscles in her neck, trying to stay awake, but it was a losing battle. She wanted to be safe inside her tree, protected by wood on all sides.

A sound startled her, but it was probably just a beetle falling from a branch into dry leaves. In an instant her fear turned to rage—to flinch at the drop of a bug that was nowhere near her was preposterous. She looked down, trying to pinpoint the beetle's location, wishing to pounce and crush and devour, to reassert her dominance over the diminutive creatures of the world, but then another one fell nearby, and then another. She wondered what could stun so many beetles at once, but then one hit her, and as she struggled to regain her balance she realized it was only rain. The drop seeped through her feathers, and she wondered how she had let the weather sneak up on her. She wondered, too—albeit briefly—how her daylit attempt at delight had turned to such lasting misery. She was now completely awake, but there was no longer any hope of hunting. She slipped from the branch and headed for home, hooting angrily at the raindrops' relentless attack.

• • •

Calvin tried to squeeze further underneath the mossy nurse log, but he couldn't find a position that would keep the rain from spattering his face. He cursed himself for forgetting a tarp. He had been afraid his father would notice if he took one from the garage ahead of time, but it had slipped his mind entirely the morning he'd made his escape. Now he was wrapped in a sodden sleeping bag with his hands crammed into his pants, trying in vain to steal more warmth from his crotch.

He had tried covering his whole head, but the blindness was unnerving. He couldn't even bring himself to face into the log for fear of what might approach him from behind.

All thoughts of his mother or of ultimate meaning were driven from his head by misery and by something that was crawling across his face. Loath to remove his hands from his groin, he tried to use telekinesis to remove the unidentified creature before it could bite. When it failed to heed his mental command but paused beside his nose, he became convinced that it was about to bite or sting, and with a spasm he pulled one hand from his pants and scrabbled at his face, rolling the bug down to his chin and crushing it, squeezing it between his fingers and flinging its body out into the rain.

Back inside the shelter of his pants, his cold, wet hand trembled and twisted, wiping bug entrails on the inside of the rough cloth. The sound of his own whimpering jerked him out of himself—he would need to be a lot tougher than this to survive. It was only rain, after all, and only a bug. He needed to accept the spattering of water on his face, the presence of centipedes and earwigs, and the crashes of approaching thunder. There was nothing he could do about them, so he'd just have to man up. He peered for a moment into the darkened trees, illuminated by increasingly frequent bursts of lightning, then shut his eyes and somehow, eventually, fell asleep.

* * *

Corwynn, surrounded by bellowing dragons, was holding her ground. Drenched and terrified, she yet screamed at each flash of light even as her screams were drowned in peals of thunder. She spun and jerked, searching the darkness for some sign of their gleaming hides, wanting to face them, wanting to attack, wanting to pull intestines from their bellies, but they remained elusive and invisible, refusing to present themselves to her fury. When the thunder at last receded, she collapsed exhausted atop her eaglets and fell into agonizing dreams wherein gigantic dragonflies pursued her under water.

12.

Ed crossed the front yard, skirting puddles, and stared at the lowest branch of the old maple tree. For years his granddaughter had begged him to put a swing up on that branch, and he had always told her he would—maybe before her next visit—but he never had. She was too old for one now, and probably wouldn't be spending much time at grandpa's house this year, but for some reason he had awoken this morning convinced it was time to fulfill his promise. He hefted a bight of rope and a length of two-by-six with two holes drilled in and cocked his head.

The tree had been old before he was born, a dependable source of spring sap and autumn gold. There had been a swing on this very branch when he was a child. The twin scars were still visible, flanked by bulging bark and darkened by last night's rain. Almost he felt he should ask permission before subjecting it to more Indian sunburns. But a promise was a promise, and he wasn't about to take *no* from a tree. So he turned his attention to figuring out a way to attach the ropes and board to the limb.

He considered fetching the stepladder but felt certain that if he thought it through he could do without. He entertained a couple ideas, rejected them, then said "Ha!" and threw a handful of coils over the branch. With a pole-vaulter's grace, the loops arced over the limb and brushed the grass with a sproing. He grabbed the dangling end and tied it to the length still in his hand, then, slick as you please, he pulled the slipknot snug against the branch. "Well, how do you like that?" he said aloud. He heard a thumping behind him and turned to Shep, who was lying in the sunshine, wagging his tail. "Why, thank you," he said, bowing slightly.

"Now, for my next trick." He threaded the rope through the holes in the board and returned to staring. With a skeptical nod, he tossed the rope's other end over the branch, pulled until the plank was roughly halfway between limb and grass, tied another slip knot, cut the excess rope with his pocketknife, then slid the seat down until it hung level. A little too high, perhaps, but a serviceable tree swing.

"You want to give her a test drive, Shep?"

Shep wagged his tail some more but made no move to get up.

"Well, while you're thinking about it . . ." He sat down and bounced once or twice, watching the branch to make sure it could handle his weight, then leaned back and started to swing.

The rope felt rough and too slender in his hands, and the small of his back tingled with the fear of being landed upon, but, as soon as he got his rhythm, somehow he was seven again, and the years between then and now evaporated like lighter fluid splashed on a summer-hot picnic table. Soon the mountain was rising overtop of the branch on the backswing, and the leaves of the limb were shushing like a giant washing machine. His stomach heaved at every downward turn, but *God*, it was nice to feel young again. The colors were more vibrant; the breeze smelled like spring. Why, if he let himself go, he'd soar clear over the mountains.

He let go. He soared almost fifteen feet before his foot caught in the grass and he flopped to the ground like a rag.

He gasped until his breath returned, and with it came a white-hot pain from his hip. He struggled to move and the pain turned blinding.

"Shit," he said, into the cool, damp grass that pressed against his face.

He lay there, lost in pain, until a cold snout pressed his neck.

"Shep," he said, in a hoarse voice. The old dog whined softly and licked his cheek.

"Good boy," he said, and closed his eyes. Pete the mailman would be by in an hour or so. Shep lay down against his side, and the raspy breathing of his ancient companion comforted him while he waited. *Good dog*, he reminded himself over and over until he passed out.

・ ・ ・

It took some time for the maple tree to piece together what had happened, but then—for only the second time in her life—she started to giggle, after the manner of maples, with a shiver of leaves and a faint scent of syrup.

・ ・ ・

Shep held himself still beside Good, struggling against the desire to bark and bite and ward off predators. But there were no predators here, just a cloud of uncertainty and an incongruously cheerful tree.

Shep hadn't been paying much attention to what Good had been doing, swinging back and forth, up and down. He didn't understand half the things the man did and generally didn't waste time trying to figure them out, but he had been surprised to see him fly.

Good had exhibited many strange and wonderful powers over the years. He could whistle like any number of birds, produce water from specific places in and around the house, and he had a Truck with which he could outrun the wind. These were marvels that never ceased to amaze, but flying surpassed them all. Shep had barked in surprise, wondering how in the world he was supposed to follow, but the flight had come to an abrupt end, leaving Good moaning and gasping and lying still.

Shep had been slow to recognize that Good was hurt. He generally assumed him to be impervious to harm. It made his heart lurch to realize that invulnerability was not in fact one of Good's powers.

So although his heart was pounding, Shep struggled to remain calm. There was nothing he could do except be with him, sharing warmth and whatever strength might flow from one body to another. Still, the fear that the last remaining member of his pack might die was overwhelming. He groaned and wished for the clarity he had felt on their walk the day before. He could think of no way to help except to lie there and bear his passing, so he put his head on his paws and stared at all the nothing that lay before him.

. . .

Calvin pulled the feathered end of the arrow to his cheek and looked down its length at the moose. He had left the trail to hunt Nazis and ninjas, but when the gigantic creature had appeared, dark brown and solid among birch trees, he had frozen, embarrassed to be seen acting silly. His plan with the arrow was to wipe any smirk off its face, but its expression was unfathomable. It seemed to be playing at being a tree.

Calvin had expected to hunt deer and rabbits, but this was the first animal he had seen bigger than a squirrel. A moose was an impractical target, but on the plus side it would be hard to miss. He licked his lips. After a day and a half of hunger, the mere sight of food—even in its rawest state—made his mouth water. His heart was beating too quickly; he couldn't be sure of his aim, the distance, or the wind, but, steeling his muscles against their trembling, he let the arrow fly.

It buried itself in leaves twenty feet short of its goal. The moose started and stamped but didn't run. Calvin drew another arrow from his quiver and began walking stealthily forward as he nocked it. The moose stared at him sideways.

Calvin focused on moving slowly and deliberately. Every sixth or seventh step, he lost his balance and wavered, but he never took his eyes off the beast. Once he crossed half the distance between them, he stopped and lifted his bow. The moose raised its head, not quite looking at him but betraying no visible sign of fear. He pulled the arrow back to his cheek and aimed for the neck.

The moment stretched as Calvin's gaze kept straying to the moose's dark brown eye.

Suddenly it lurched, splayed its front legs, and lowered its antlers. Calvin flinched without letting go of the arrow. It looked absurdly like a dog that wants to play. Then, realizing that the moose's pose was probably an attack stance, he belatedly loosed the arrow, which floated harmlessly over the moose's head. It snorted, and Calvin—fumbling to draw another arrow—turned and fled.

He couldn't tell, over the sound of his own crashing steps, whether the moose was following him, and he didn't dare look back. He saw a thick copse of trees and dashed for it, imagining the moose snorting and snarling at his back. He dove into the thicket and turned. The moose was where he had left it, prancing, shuffling, and huffing. As he leaned against one of the trees, struggling to breathe, he remembered throwing his bow to the ground in panic. "Fuck," he said. He couldn't see where it had landed, so he decided to wait until the moose went away before retrieving it.

As he watched the moose nibble placidly at bushes and nose the dirt, Calvin replayed their confrontation over and over. He imagined how his first shot might have plunged into its eye. Racing alongside the crazed and bleeding behemoth, he nocked another arrow, diving sideways and shooting the second arrow into its flank, a third into its neck, and he was up and running as the gigantic beast, weak from lack of blood and confused by pain, slowly crumpled to its knees, thundered onto its side, and breathed its last. Dad would mount the moose's head above the fireplace, displacing Shawn's marlin from their Florida vacation two years ago.

He savored the image but couldn't keep it from reminding him that he had left his home, his father, and his brother and was living alone in the woods. He tried to imagine retrieving the bow and killing the moose, building a fire beside its body and living for weeks off the meat, using its hide for a blanket, carving spear points from its rack. He tried to imagine it realistically, in every detail—and to imagine that he could actually accomplish it. But as stiff as he imagined his resolve to be, he continued to sit and muse and watch the moose, and to imagine how proud his father would be if he killed it and brought it home.

By the time the sun had passed its zenith, the moose had not moved more than fifty feet. It looked as though it planned to spend the whole day there. Calvin sat with his back against a tree trunk and tried not to think of anything. Birdsong lulled him toward drowsiness, and the mazy sunlight shimmering through the leaves eased his mind. He began to notice his breathing and even his pulse. Though the moose remained a constant presence in his mind, it ceased to seem like a threat. He even began to feel a certain kinship with it. He was like a wild animal himself, now, lonely and free.

13.

Ed picked at the dinner the nurse had brought, but he wasn't all that hungry, and the food wasn't very good. Pete had found him, tugged an uncooperative Shep inside, and called an ambulance. Not long after he arrived at the hospital, the doctor told him he'd dislocated his hip. They'd dosed him with pain killers and relocated it. He'd been feeling pretty good before they brought his supper.

"How do you feel, Dad?" said Mary, leaning over him like a robin seeking worms.

Ed tried to cover his surprise with a smile. The nurse who admitted him had asked for his nearest relative, and he had given Mary's name and phone number, but he hadn't expected her to drive all the way out here.

"Foolish," he said, attempting to laugh.

"Foolish? Why? Dad, what happened?"

"Ah, well. You know that swing I've been promising Lissy since she was little?"

"... Not really."

"Well..."

"Well, what?"

Ed chuckled. "I jumped."

Mary's eyes went wide. "Dad! You're—What? You jumped off a *swing?* Are you fucking crazy? What were you thinking?"

"I guess I was thinking it would be fun."

"Fun?" She pursed her lips and looked away, the very picture of Karen. "I assumed you . . . fell off a ladder or something. It never occurred to me you'd . . ."

After a moment she said, her voice strangely hesitant, "Dad, it's not good for you to be alone out there all by yourself."

"Ah," he turned his head to the window.

"Dad." She paused, and Ed closed his eyes, preparing for the worst. "I think Lissy should come stay with you, just for a few weeks, until your hip heals."

Ed looked at her, squinting, taken off guard. "Well . . . that would be—I mean—great. I'd love to have Lissy spend the summer; of course she can. But what then? You gonna commit me to a nursing home?"

Mary turned her head, apparently fighting back tears.

"All right," he said. "Never mind. If Lissy wants to move in with her old granddad for a few weeks, let her come. I could use the help."

"It's for the best," said Mary.

"Just so long as Lissy thinks so, too. I don't want her resenting me all summer."

"Of course she won't resent you."

He thought a moment. "Well, then, good," he said, forcefully, still trying to sort things out. He took her hand (*careful*, whispered his hip) and squeezed a little, smiling. "It's good to see you, Mary."

"Good to see you, too, Dad."

○ ○ ○

Shep's dream is a memory from long ago. Pumpkin's whelp, Lissy, is hitting him with a stick. She does not seem angry; in fact, she's yipping playfully, but she's playing too rough. He waits for an opening and nips Lissy's hand to teach her a lesson about hurting. He does not bite hard—barely enough to break the skin—but Lissy yelps and runs away.

Good has not yet become the old friend he is now, though he has been kind, affectionate, and a skilled provider. But now he is striding across the yard, howling angrily. He picks up the stick that Lissy dropped and hits him with it much harder than Lissy had. Instantly, Shep rolls over and shows his belly, letting Good know he is sorry, and acknowledging him as pack leader, but Good ignores this act of submission, as well as his whimpers. Under repeated blows, pain and terror overwhelm his obedience, and Shep rolls to his feet and bolts. Good chases him, barking ferociously and waving the stick over his head. The ground heaves with bewildered panic, but Shep dares not stumble. He finds a thick stand of bushes and desperately crawls underneath them. Eventually, Good leaves off his barking and returns home, leaving Shep to lick his bruises.

Late the next day Shep will return to the pack, because he is hungry and has nowhere else to go. Good will be in his chair, and Shep will limp toward him to lick his hand. Good will say kind words and pat him on the head. But for now there is only roaring pain, yawning exile, and the understanding that Lissy's well-being is infinitely more precious than his own.

Shep woke up, twitching from remembered pain, and looked around for Good, wishing to seek forgiveness one more time. Then he remembered that Good was not there. He sighed, wondering how long it would take him to starve to death.

* * *

Mary waved off the attendant and pushed her father's wheelchair out to the car herself. Likewise, her father waved off her help in getting inside. She watched him anxiously until he was clicking his seatbelt, then closed the door and returned the wheelchair to the emergency-room doors.

They drove in silence, interrupted by occasional stabs at small talk. The familiar awkwardness comforted Mary and eased her fear that he was heading for dementia. They talked about how wet the weather had been lately; they made plans for Mary to drop off Lissy the next day; and they watched the houses and sidewalks give way to trees.

As always, she felt a mounting nostalgia as she neared her childhood home. Every house, every curve in the road, affected her like a recurring dream. There was the red house with weathered black shutters that stood too close to the road. There was the post office, its brick walls out of place among so much clapboard. There was the cemetery. Her best friend Jane had warned her to hold her breath whenever she passed it, and to put a finger in her navel to keep the ghosts out.

Mary exhaled when they were safely past, and glanced at her father to see if he'd noticed. He was staring straight ahead, lips pressed firmly together, bracing his body against every bump and sway. With a guilty start she checked the speedometer and discovered how fast she was driving. She eased off the accelerator and coasted to a gentler speed, forcing herself to ignore the memories and focus instead on ameliorating the impact of the road's many bumps and curves. Out of the corner of her eye she watched her father slowly relax.

At last they were crossing the bridge and taking the last turn. The old road was rutted and pot-holed in exactly the same places. She seemed to remember every pebble. When the house came into view, she was surprised, as always, to find it smaller than she remembered. The old pickup was parked by the tree, and Mom's azaleas were in bloom. The only substantial change was the swing dangling from the maple tree. She shook her head, half in wonder, half in disapproval, then backed the car up to the door.

It was slow going, but she managed to help him into the house and get him settled in his favorite chair. Shep was excited to see them both, but seemed interested mainly in licking Dad's hand. Mary felt an odd pang. Usually, when she visited, Shep focused all his attention on her, but today the old dog took no notice of her attempts to scratch his ear. Wherever Dad's hand went, Shep was twisting to lick it, till his head was sideways on the arm of the recliner, his tongue reaching for the hand that Dad had pulled into his lap.

"Do you want Shep in the kitchen, Dad?"

"No," he said, shortly, his pain audible. "He's alright. Shep's a . . . good dog."

Another pang. This time she recognized it as jealousy. Dad would get to spend the next few weeks with Lissy and Shep, while she would be all alone. She considered suggesting a trade—the girl for the dog—but thought better of it. She fetched a glass of water, a jar of peanuts, and his cordless phone and put them on the table beside him, next to his pain pills. She kissed him on the forehead and told him she'd be back tomorrow afternoon with Lissy.

She felt guilty leaving him but wanted to get home as quickly as possible, so she could start acclimating Lissy to her new summer plans.

14.

Æthel had neither slept nor eaten for two days. Upon reflection, she decided it had been a mistake to desire acceptance from her fellow creatures, thereby counting herself a part of some larger family. It made killing and eating her cousins problematic. A porcupine trundled from one tree to another not far away, but instead of wondering how to clutch its neck without getting stabbed, she found herself imagining what it was like to have quills, and how she would defend herself from an aerial assault if she did. It was unnerving. Even mice and shrews seemed like vulnerable, valuable creatures with as much right to enjoy the night as she. As the stars wheeled slowly overhead, she grew more and more absorbed by the lives of the creatures around her. Her hunger all but forgotten, she listened to their scritchings and scratchings, and imagined herself nosing under leaves for insects or nibbling tender grasses and succulent leaf buds. By the time the darkness began to withdraw, she was drunk with empathy and lightheaded from lack of food. A vague anxiety began to steal over her; if she didn't eat soon, she would become too weak to hunt. Even more worrisome, she might become too weak to fly home.

• • •

In the grayish light of approaching dawn, Calvin sat braced between branches, squinting. He thought he could make out something large sitting in a tree some fifty feet away. Maybe a turkey. He pulled up the bow and sighted the bird along the arrow. Summoning all his patience, he waited for it to take flight. In a moment, to his surprise, it started flying right toward him. He pulled the arrow farther back, waited two seconds more and let loose. The arrow caught the bird in the shoulder, and suddenly it was a great horned owl, twisting and falling soundlessly. As soon as it hit the ground, it started thrashing, struggling to escape the arrow's bite.

At last the owl went still for a moment, lying on its side in the paling light. Slowly its mouth opened—impossibly wide—and emitted a long, whistling scream.

· · ·

Corwynn's hackles rose, and she covered the half-eaten fish with her wings, instinctively wanting to protect it from whatever could cause an owl such pain. Panic urged her to fly away, as far and as fast as possible, but fear no longer ruled her, and it was quickly replaced by rage, which calmly suggested she confront the owl's attacker and, if possible, deliver the owl from its claws.

She launched herself at the trees, scanning the forest's edge for points of entry, but there were none. She balked at the last instant and landed, her head bobbing up and down, searching for some way in that would accommodate her wings. The realization that she would have to walk filled her with a creeping dread but did nothing to blunt her resolve. The first few steps were manageable, but the hard fact was that her feet were not made for walking. They could clutch, perch and rend with perfect efficiency, but they were never intended for locomotion.

Steeling herself against defeat, Corwynn lifted each leg with exaggerated care and picked her way through the clawing underbrush.

The strangeness of the forest was appalling; it was dark as an approaching storm, and humongous shapes loomed menacingly. Before long her legs were burning with pain.

Again the owl cried out, a pained, descending, "Hroo-oo-oo" that broke her heart. She launched into flight, fearing to arrive too late, but was immediately faced with a copse too dense to fly through and too broad to fly around. She veered, but other trees confused her and she landed.

Once more she walked, concentrating on the direction of the owl's cries, her progress impossibly slow. She strained to stare through the trees but had no idea how far the owl might be. The cry had seemed loud, even over the noise of the river, but now the forest was quiet, as though the owl didn't really exist, as though she were walking through a dream.

Just as she was thinking the nightmare would never end, she stepped on something soft that wheezed. She stepped backward and peered at the ground. Her tired eyes had trouble distinguishing the feathers of a great horned owl from the similarly colored leaves upon which she lay. What Corwynn could see was a long, unnaturally straight stick protruding from the owl's shoulder. The red tip gleamed dully. When glowing orange eyes opened slowly, she feared the bird's neck must be broken until she remembered the unnerving ability of owls to spin their head around.

She clicked her beak against the other's to reassure her. In response, the owl only blinked, more slowly than Corwynn would have thought possible. Gently, with almost the same care she had used to free her son from his egg, she grabbed the stick with her mouth. The owl tensed, but did not jerk or cry out. She bit down with steady pressure until the wooden shaft crunched and split in two. While she struggled to dislodge the pieces from her beak with her tongue, the owl lurched to her feet like a startled cow and started worrying the black feathers that protruded like a growth from under her shoulder. Corwynn issued a soft screech and flapped her wings to distract her, then leaned in to take the disturbing tuft in her mouth. When she pulled, the owl's eyes went wide and she stumbled backward. The black stick slid out of her shoulder like a hideous worm. The owl looked down at her wound, where dark blood matted her feathers. She looked back at Corwynn mournfully.

Just then a crash startled them both. Corwynn spun to face a human who had apparently just dropped from a tree. She raised her wings and hissed, prepared to strike should it rush her, but once it took a backward step her every feather urged her to flee. Out of the corner of her eye she saw the owl stumbling awkwardly, trailing her hurt wing. Her mind told her the owl was beyond help, but her heart and wings said otherwise. Nearly blind with panic, she leaped upon the owl, dug her claws into her shoulders, and lifted her—barely noticing her renewed cries of pain—before racing for the river. Impossibly, she navigated the menacing trees and came at length to the banks, where she dropped the owl and fled for her nest, desperate to make sure her eaglets were safe. She winced when she heard the splash behind her but would not allow herself to look back.

She had done the best she could.

. . .

Æthel washed downstream like a clump of leaves, contorting her neck to keep her beak above water as her body bashed into rocks and her talons scraped the sandy bottom. Her wings were more intent on dragging her under than lifting her up, so she let them flail limply in the icy current. Her wound was a beehive of pain, and she quickly became impatient for the river to swallow her.

Instead, the water slowed, and the cold seemed to ease. With a tremendous and inspired twist of her body, she managed to get her belly above water, her wings stretched out on either side, as if she were soaring upside down. This made it easier to breathe, allowing her to relax just a little, but it also turned the world inside out: while she soared through water, clouds and branches circled haphazardly below her.

Soon the pain ceased to focus on her shoulder and instead formed a general brightness that was one with the sunlight and water. She grew tired, and her wings began to bend.

Just as her mind was slipping toward sleep—her beak about to dip underwater—a sudden vision of the stick that had leapt like a lightning bolt out of a tree jolted her awake with a splash. With the focus that terror sometimes brings, she maintained her awkward balance.

She had never known a tree to lash out like that, had never seen one move without aid from the wind. And, too, she had never known an eagle to come to another creature's aid. Had she been out in the open, it would not have surprised her to be eaten by an eagle in such a state, but beneath trees only crows and foxes should have savaged her carcass, and then only after she was safely dead.

The world seemed robbed of all sense, and so in time she might have died bewildered, had the river not pushed her into a deadfall of brush and leaves. How she managed to clamber up onto it with limbs gone numb she didn't know, but the blessed relief of lying on her breast in the still, dry air, panting and trembling, was a feeling that would come to her in dreams long after the traumatic visions of attacking trees faded away.

○ ○ ○

Calvin stared after the birds for a long time. The wonder they stirred within him was an emotion he could study at leisure without its diminishing. His insides seemed to have opened up from a narrow tunnel into a vast, underground chamber; the world was not as dull as he had been led to believe. It was like those books his mother had used to read to him and Shawn, where animals talked and heroes went on dangerous quests to kill dragons.

The thought came to him slowly—as if from outside himself—that he should follow the birds. As soon as it arrived, he realized he should have run after them immediately, but he had been too conflicted—torn between driving the eagle away from his prey and protecting himself should the birds attack—to pay any attention to the bizarreness of the encounter. By now they were long gone.

Still—he had nowhere else to be—why not follow in the general direction they had flown and hope to catch up? Who knows to what kingdom of noble birds they might lead him? As if in a dream, he snatched his pack and the bow and quiver from the base of the tree and started walking.

He stopped when he reached the river, and tried to decide if he should wade right across or walk upstream where more numerous rocks might allow a dry crossing. Downstream, he reasoned, could only lead him back to human habitations, and wet shoes are annoying to walk in, so upstream he headed.

After a few steps, however, he felt a strange tug, like a phantom hand on his shoulder urging him back. He tried to shake the feeling, assuming it was only gravity, but it wouldn't leave. At last he stopped and stared at the water, puzzled. In truth the brook was only babbling incomprehensibly, but in his mind it was saying *Follow me*. And why not? What did he really expect to find up slope? With a shrug, he released his magical raptor fantasies and chose instead the path of least resistance.

Twenty minutes later, a brush pile in the middle of the stream caught his attention. Something about the clump of leaves on top seemed odd—moist and masticated. As soon as he realized it might be a wet and bedraggled owl, he stepped into the stream without further thought and splashed across to it. It was face down, with scrawny-looking wings splayed out on either side, and he couldn't tell if its back rose and fell with the rhythm of breathing or the pulsing of the stream. Gingerly, he turned it over. Its eyes were closed, but when he touched its breast, he could feel a rapid heartbeat. He gathered its wings and lifted the owl, amazed at how light it was, and waded back to the bank to sit down and study it.

He was hoping to be awestruck by the fact of holding a wild owl. He wanted to become entranced by each wet feather. Instead, he was repulsed by its funky smell and disturbed by the fact that it hardly looked like an owl at all—more like a wet rat with a hooked beak and a skinny neck. Despite his hunger, it looked not the least bit appetizing.

He couldn't figure out why the eagle had "rescued" the owl only to drop it in the river, but it made about as much sense as anything else. He had to admit that a part of him had been happy to choose the downhill route, because, so long as he wasn't actively searching for a magical city of birds, he could allow some part of himself to believe it was really there. But here was solid evidence that no such city existed. It was stupid to feel disappointed in such an obvious fact, but disappointed he was. Shawn was right: The world is a shithole and nothing much matters.

He considered dropping the limp clump in the river and moving along, but then he thought how cool it would be to have a great horned owl as a pet. He could walk around with it perched on his shoulder like a pirate's parrot. He could teach it to hunt rabbits for him. It would be better than just wandering out in the woods all alone until he starved to death.

One of his hands had a trace of watery blood on it, so he took off his shirt, wrapped the owl in it and decided to take it to a vet.

15.

Ed woke up feeling remarkably comfortable. The pain in his hip was barely noticeable, no worse than if he'd slept too long in the recliner. Now that his hip was back where it belonged, he'd be dancing a jig in no time. As much as he was looking forward to Lissy's visit, he considered calling Mary to let her know that Lissy's services would not be required. Then he pulled the lever on the side of the chair to bring himself upright and yelped. Shep answered from the floor beside him.

Ed held himself still, willing the pain to recede, but it wouldn't back off. "Well, this won't do," he whispered through clenched teeth. He grabbed his cane and forced himself to his feet. Tears came to his eyes, and he could only breathe in gasps, but he refused to give in to the pain. If he allowed himself to sit back down and recline into a comfortable position, he'd not have the courage to stand up again for the rest of the day. Blowing like a woman in labor, he hobble-hopped to the kitchen. Leaning on the counter, he let his injured leg hang free and gingerly tried to stretch it. The pain eased slightly, but nowhere near enough. "Ah, crap," he said, as he realized that the pain pills were still on the table beside his chair. "Fetch the pills, Shep."

Shep cocked his head and lifted his ears. He had followed Ed dutifully back into the kitchen, but Lassie he was not. Ed shook his head. If he walked back to the chair he was sure to sit down in it, and Mary and Lissy were due to arrive in a couple of hours. He couldn't bear for them to see him sitting invalid. Once his breathing was under control, he renewed his grip on the cane and decided to challenge the pain to a duel.

Somehow, he managed to get to the door, hold it open for Shep and get himself down three steps and into the yard.

Oddly enough, the walk did him some good. By the time he circled the house twice—pausing to relieve his bladder into the azaleas—his hip was no worse than when he'd left the hospital. He was breathing more easily, and some of the tension was abating. When he passed the swing, he took hold of the rope to give it an affectionate shake, stepped wrong, cried out, and knew he had but moments before he collapsed. "Shit," he said, but he managed to ease himself into the swing. Unfortunately, he couldn't find a way to give all his weight to the wooden board, so he let himself slide to the ground. He tried to put his weight into the ropes at his armpits, but that wasn't going to work, either. With a heavy sigh, he slid the rest of the way out of the swing and lay flat on his back, while the swing did what swings do best above his torso.

Shep lay down beside him as though nothing were out of the ordinary. "Just another day on the Nowlen Farm, eh, Shep?"

Slowly, gently, he reached a hand into a pocket and retrieved his cigarette pack and lighter.

• • •

In his dream, Shep is caught in a tangle of undergrowth, more concerned with the scent he can almost smell than with extricating himself. As briars claw past his fur and thick stems impede his progress, his nose strains at the odor that may not really be there at all. Who is it? All he knows for sure is that it is person rather than prey—and not quite a stranger. But who? The aroma is as close as his tail, but he can't quite catch it.

Suddenly the branches and tendrils give way, and he slides through the brush into the faint yet unpleasant whiff of—but no—it belongs to a stranger after all . . .

Shep awoke with a tiny, startled *woof*. He scanned the area, alert for danger, and saw a human traipsing toward them through the field. He heaved himself to his feet and growled. The sound surprised him; he hadn't growled in ages. He glanced at Good, who was still on his back, then returned his attention to the intruder. The angles of the boy's stride spoke of stress. He carried a bundle in front of him the way Ed used to carry chickens. A small gust of wind brought more of the scent that had awoken him, confirming the stress and revealing wet owl and the boy's identity. He was akin to a man Good sometimes talked to when he went into town, whom Shep had never liked, though Good always shook his hand and laughed when he talked to him. But that didn't give this overgrown puppy permission to trespass.

• • •

When Shep barked, Ed looked up and saw a bare-chested teenager walking toward them. He was still a little ways off, so Ed grabbed his cane and, between that and the swing, managed to pull himself up. The pain was almost bearable, but he couldn't quite get all the way upright, so he settled for sitting in the swing and waiting for the stranger to arrive.

The boy stopped in front of Shep, who had gone out to meet him and was sniffing his pants. Ed leaned forward, trying to make out what the bundle was that the boy was lifting out of Shep's reach. Shep's tail was waving slowly as he breathed in what must have been, from the look of the boy's pants, a veritable banquet of smells.

Suddenly, the bundle started writhing. Talons appeared in front of the dog's nose. Shep stepped backward and started barking hoarsely. It was all the boy could do to hang onto what was suddenly an enormous bird, some kind of hawk, maybe.

Given a pressing reason to stand, Ed found he could ignore the ruthless stab of pain long enough to do so. "What have you got there, son?" he called.

He waited while the two performed an oddly graceful dance until the boy pulled the bird close to his chest, and the bird, in response, went limp.

Ed took another step forward, then asked again, "I said, 'What you got there, son?'"

The boy closed his mouth and swallowed, his eyes scanning the ground. "It's an owl."

"So it is," said Ed, seeing it clearly in an instant. "How'd you come by it?"

Straightening his posture, the boy stuck out his chin and looked Ed straight in the eye. "I shot it."

Ed couldn't tell if the boy was bragging or just brazenly telling the truth in an awkward moment. There was a bow slung across his shoulder.

Ed puckered his lips and nodded. "Bothering you, was it?"

"What?"

"The owl. Bothering you?"

"No," the boy said, looking disconcerted. Ed just stared. "No, I—" he put his head down. "Not really. It's lost some blood."

The shame in the boy's voice softened Ed's attitude toward him somewhat. "I imagine it has. You got a name, son?" he asked.

"Calvin."

"Well, Calvin, I'm Ed. Ed Nowlen." Nodding at the bow, he said, "I guess you're a pretty good shot with that bow."

Calvin blushed. "It was just luck," he said. "Dumb luck, I guess."

Ed chuckled politely. "Well, just don't point that thing in my direction, okay? I've got plenty of dumb luck to go around."

"All right," said Calvin.

Ed looked hard at him, debating whether or not to reveal the next flash of insight. "You're Frank Berman's son, aren't you?"

The boy paled, looking as though he wanted to run. With apparent difficulty he got himself under control. "Yeah," he said.

Ed stepped forward, hoping the boy wouldn't mistake his grimace for anger. "Let's get your owl wrapped up, so it doesn't go anywhere, and then get you something to eat." He led Calvin very slowly to the barn and held the door open for him. "How long has it been since the last time you ate?"

"Uhhh," said Calvin

"That's what I figured. Grab that feed sack over there, will you? And the loop of baling twine. All right, gently now."

Together they peeled Calvin's shirt off the owl, rewrapped it in burlap and set it on the floor. "There," said Ed. "As fine a straitjacket as any owl could hope for. Now let's get out of here before Shep drags himself in and takes an interest." They left the barn, and Ed propped a length of wood against the door to keep it closed. "My granddaughter's arriving in a little bit, and we want you looking presentable when she gets here."

Calvin seemed taken aback but said nothing. Ed clapped him on the shoulder and pushed him toward the house, too busy ignoring the wracking pain in his hip to acknowledge that he was getting into something more complicated than caring for a wounded owl.

Æthel had only had flashes of consciousness since the deadfall, but each flash was more alarming than the last. In the first, she was floating above a meadow of tall grasses, wrapped in something that smelled outrageous, and pursued by something whose breathing was almost as loud as its footfalls. She had been about to turn her head to look when she noticed she was already in the creature's grasp and promptly passed out again. The second time, she was bounding through pine trees, still wrapped, still clutched, still pursued, but the place was familiar: The light was too bright for absolute certainty, but she was convinced her own tree was only a short flight away. She attempted to escape, but the talons around her torso, though blunt, were implacable; she passed out again. The third time she was weaving improbably through the air faced with a large dog. That time, she had put all her strength into lashing out, but to no avail; she had passed out again, assuming she was about to be eaten. Instead, she had awoken in a dark, cool, cavernous enclosure, wrapped in something that smelled more of plant than mammal, and she was completely alone.

She turned her head around, just to make sure, but behind her was only wood. She tried to spread her wings, but they were pinned to her sides. It was just as well; the simple effort of trying caused her shoulder unbearable pain. She was too weak to fly far anyway.

She wondered what death was waiting for.

· · ·

Calvin sat at the kitchen table and tried not to fidget. He was ready to give up his dream of a pet owl and be on his way, but this old man he only vaguely recognized was limping around, fixing him a sandwich. If not for the fact that he hadn't eaten anything at all the last couple days, he would have bolted. He certainly had no desire to be there when the guy's granddaughter showed up.

"You like lettuce?" the guy asked.

"Sure."

"Tomato?"

"Yeah."

"Mayo or mustard?"

"Either."

"How about a little of both?"

"Okay."

When the sandwich was placed in front of him, Calvin barely managed to say "Thanks," before shoving half of it into his mouth. It was the best thing he had ever tasted.

"How about another one?"

Calvin nodded.

He ate the second one a little slower, savoring it, but before he was finished he heard a car door slam, and then another. He stood up, wondering how to reach the back door, but a hand fell on his shoulder, surprisingly strong, pushing him back into his seat.

"No need to rush. Finish eating."

His heart hammering—no longer able to chew, let alone swallow—Calvin stared at the door as though the Gestapo were about to kick it in.

16.

Ed noticed Mary's smile go tight around the edges but was surprised when she pulled him into the dining room and hissed, "Are you crazy?" He struggled to ride out the waves of pain from his hip while trying to figure out why his daughter was angry.

"Did you think about Lissy before you so graciously opened your home to this, this runaway? Did the fact that your granddaughter—"

"Calvin? He's Frank Berman's kid. And he's got nowhere to go. It's not like he's some dangerous criminal."

"Fine. Well, I guess Lissy can just stay home this summer."

Ed looked at the tears welling in his daughter's eyes and tried to work out a response. The thought of Mary taking Lissy back home cut his heart, which made him feel panicked and defensive, which in turn made him feel manipulated and angry. Through gritted teeth, he said, "Well, if that's how you feel . . ."

But now she was weeping, falling against his chest like she was nine, like when they'd put Mittens to sleep. He held her awkwardly, remembering that he'd felt just as full of resentment and shame back then. Mary had flown at him in a rage, and he had felt like the troll under the bridge until she broke down crying and hugged him just this way. It reminded him, then as now, that he was her father, and that she still loved him, even if he did do cruel and unfathomable things sometimes.

"Oh, Pumpkin," he said.

Immediately she pulled away from him and swiped away her tears. "I need a break, Dad. I take care of her all year round, all by myself, and I don't even know how I take care of myself sometimes. I thought she could help you out, that it could work out to everyone's advantage, but now . . ."

They both stood silent, lost in the moment's misery.

"It'll be okay, Mary. I promise."

Mary let one more tear fall, then stared at a corner of the ceiling. At last her shoulders sagged.

"It better be," she said.

. . .

Shep was ecstatic. The arrival of Son with the owl had been interesting, but this—the pack reassembled—was beyond his wildest dreams. The only one missing was Kare Bear, but Pumpkin was back and Shep's heart was aflutter. She was old enough now to be the pack's dam, and Lissy! He hastened to her and suffered himself to be petted.

Abruptly the memory of his dream returned, and he was shocked to discover that he had never completely forgiven her. For a moment his whole body trembled with an effort not unlike vomiting, but soon enough he felt the release, the purging, and immediately he felt better. He leaned into her and sighed, licking her other hand.

She was too busy investigating Son to pay much attention, but her hand stayed on his head. It was enough.

. . .

When Calvin shrugged again, Lissy considered slapping him. Every question she asked he answered with the same monotonal "I don't know," or atonal shrug.

She tried again. "Were you going to eat it, or . . ." She rolled her hand, inviting him to elaborate, but he wouldn't even look her in the eyes. She turned to Shep, whom she'd been idly stroking. "I bet you would have eaten it, wouldn't you?" Shep at least had the social grace to stare deep into her eyes and wag his tail, even if he didn't exactly answer the question.

She looked at the wall clock that was also a dinner plate, and wondered how much longer Mom intended to agonize over the decision to leave her there with these two strange men. She was pretty sure the poor woman was crying by now.

"It's a great horned owl," said Calvin, startling Lissy after the period of silence.

She recovered quickly. "Oh," she said, perhaps a little condescendingly, as if Calvin were six instead of older than her. But what else was she supposed to make of this little tidbit, except that Calvin was perhaps not all that bright?

The renewed silence was starting to ring in her ears by the time Mom and Grandpa came back to the kitchen. Sure enough, her eyes looked a bit red and puffy.

"Hey, Mom! Calvin shot an owl. With an arrow. It has great horns."

"Wow," said Mom, vaguely trying to look impressed, though Lissy suspected she would have reacted the same way to news that Calvin was from Mars, or had eaten a bag of chips for lunch.

"So, are you still going to leave me here, or what?"

Lissy would have felt better if her mother had given her a weary, hurt look instead of turning pale and muttering something like, "You'll be fine, hon." With a shock, Lissy realized two things—that Mom really was worried about leaving her there, and that she was doing it anyway.

Mom was kissing her on the cheek while she thought these things, saying goodbye to Grandpa and "Nice to meet you" to Calvin, and she was gone before Lissy could figure out how upset this realization made her.

She had a full minute to stare at the door before her granddad said, "Shall we check in on Mr. Owl?" Lissy turned to him slowly, her mouth still open in shock. "Okay," she said, just as slowly, but whether in response to his question or to her mother leaving, she wasn't sure.

. . .

Æthel's wounded wing was a babbling river of pain, but that and her hunger were the only things convincing her she was still alive. The smells that surrounded her were of dead wood, dung, and dry grass: ancient odors, as though no rain had fallen here in many a season, nor was there any breath of wind. Bats squeaked sleepily overhead, but the skin in which she was wrapped precluded any thought of hunting.

Presently, a hole appeared some distance before her, letting in a temporarily blinding flash of light. When it closed, three humans were staring at her with tiny eyes.

The one in front rumbled, pointing a blunt talon as all three advanced. Æthel turned her head and closed her eyes, as if protecting her face from a fierce north wind.

The ground squeaked and growled at their approach, sending shivers up her legs. She tried to remain calm and accept her fate philosophically, but the predators were moving so slowly that before long she lost all control, hissing and convulsing, hopping pathetically, wings straining, until, twisting awkwardly, she toppled sideways, her breast on the ground but her face toward the humans, beak agape, hissing like a possum.

She barely registered that the tallest one was sheathing its blunt claws in another layer of skin, that it was crouching and kneeling, one claw outstretched, sheathed talons turned inward. The creature loomed like fear itself, and yet its claw hung fire at Æthel's open beak so long that her panic had no choice but to crumple in upon itself. It was as if she was being asked to trust, and, although she could not let go of her fear, Æthel managed at last to close her beak and swallow.

※ ※ ※

"That's right," said Ed, in what he hoped was a soothing tone of voice, keeping his hand still for a few moments longer. He didn't know much about owls, but with the animals he did know, swallowing was a good sign. He hoped so, because if the owl decided to bite down on one of his fingers he was going to lose that finger, leather glove or no. Hardly daring to breathe—trying to inject a confidence he didn't feel into his every movement—he reached his hands around the owl's body and lifted it up, pressing it into his belly. His main concern was that the beak be out of range of his neck. He was prepared for a struggle, but the owl, though tense, made no effort to escape.

"Okay, now. Careful of the beak. Don't give him a shot at any of your fingers. Just put a piece of that ground beef on the palm of your hand and hold it up where he can reach it. Nice and easy."

It was Calvin's glove that first hovered in front of the owl's beak with a wad of beef on the palm, but its eyes were closed again, and it took no notice of the meat. Calvin lifted his hand, and Ed wanted to shout at him not to force it, but the boy had already mashed the meat onto the hook of the beak, where it stuck. Calvin pulled his hand away, laughing horsishly.

"That's enough," said Ed. "Take it off." But it was Lissy who reached in and removed the beef, and she wasn't wearing a glove. Ed had somehow forgotten how much common sense kids lack. Gritting his teeth, he tried to keep his voice calm as he said, "Lissy, don't put your fingers near the beak without wearing gloves." But Lissy was already deftly sliding the meat into owl's open mouth and stroking its neck, as if she'd been working with raptors her whole life. Convulsively, it swallowed and opened its eyes. Ed cleared his throat.

"Well, uh, that was nicely done, Lissy."

"Thanks," she said, brightly.

"Yeah, great job," said Calvin.

Ed couldn't tell if the boy's praise was sincere.

"Well. Since you're so good with owls, why don't you hold out its wing while Calvin sprays its wound with water."

Awkwardly, they managed to pull off enough of the burlap to free its wing, which Lissy stretched out full. Again, the owl convulsed, undoubtedly in pain, but Lissy hushed it, saying, "It's okay, Mr. Horns," and stroking its head with her free hand. Its wing was impressively large, almost as long as Ed's arm. It was matted with caked blood, and Ed was sorry he hadn't done this earlier.

"Okay, Calvin. You're up."

Calvin held the spray bottle like a pistol and fired several streams of water at the wound, making gun noises as he did. Ed looked at Lissy for a raised eyebrow, but she was staring intently at the wound. "Get under it more," she said. "That stuff's just blood, it's not where the arrow went in."

At the mention of the arrow, Calvin seemed to get more serious, and he trained the streams of water a little lower down.

"Yeah. Right there," said Lissy.

Ed looked at his granddaughter with wonder and newfound respect. She reminded him of some of the nurses he'd met in the war. After some fumbling, and a couple of false tries, she wrapped the owl's good wing to its side with a clean strip of bed linen, then folded the wounded wing in over the cloth, and wrapped it all together three more times. She used a couple of clips from an ace bandage to attach the end. All the while, the owl suffered itself to be manipulated and struggled no more.

At last Ed placed it back on the floor and stood back to admire their handiwork. "Not a bad job," he said. "As good a straitjacket as an owl could hope for."

"You said that last time," said Calvin.

Ed looked at him sidelong. "Sure," he said.

...

Kyron was almost asleep when a sharp noise near the door of his cage startled him. It was too late for any humans to be wandering about, and although he had never glimpsed the giant spiders that wove the gleaming gray webs, he had grown accustomed to the sounds the strands made, the clinks and jangles. These sounds were louder—somehow violent—and Kyron grew concerned. After several repetitions a human figure appeared at the back of the cage, crouched and mysterious. Kyron flew up to the highest of his perches, and watched as the figure lifted its spindly wings and called up to him softly.

Kyron looked away, resolved to ignore it, but then his perch began, ever so slightly, to tremble. He leaped upward in alarm and barely caught himself on the wing. The human was attempting to shake his tree. He hovered for a moment, his rage surging as he furiously flapped. He considered diving at the human to drive it away, but he mastered himself, flew to the other branch and turned his face away once more.

When some time had passed without further commotion, he looked down. The human was staring up at him. As he watched, it spread its upper limbs slightly and then convulsed, emitting a short cough.

Kyron blinked. There was something familiar about the gesture, something that made his heart race. After a moment, he made the connection: it was the way many creatures, such as deer, had of raising the alarm. Again, Kyron blinked, uncertain. Creatures in nearby cages were beginning to stir, nervous and agitated. The human growled and walked to the intersection of two webs.

Unexpectedly, it began to climb. As Kyron watched, it made its ungainly way to the top. With one hand it slowly reached back to scratch its rump. When it pulled its hand away, it was holding something Kyron hadn't seen before. Whatever it was, the human brought it to the top web, where it produced the same twanging sounds that had preceded the intruder's entrance. Kyron raised his head, suddenly more alert. He craned his neck, trying to get a better view. Was there another opening? He had worried the strands all around with beak and claws to no avail. What did this human sense that Kyron could not? Kyron flew to the other perch to get a closer look. The human turned around when he landed, but Kyron dipped his head to indicate that it should continue its work. The human hunched its neck and returned to twanging.

Patiently, the human applied the implement to one strand after another, slowly shifting its position when it could no longer reach the next one. It continued—its breath becoming steadily more labored—until finally it was able to push the corner of the upper web straight up and actually climb out. It stood atop Kyron's enclosure and let out an eerily owl-like call. Kyron gazed in surprise as the human's intentions became clear, shocked at the effort it had expended on his behalf. He hesitated only a moment, then leapt through the opening and on, and up, and into the boundless night. The human cried out as he flew, and this time the call sounded like nothing so much as the howling of a wolf.

17.

"-n down to Eagle Point Motors! Let our American eagle point you toward the car of your drea-"

Mary slapped the alarm clock and then froze. "Lissy. Oh God."

She heaved herself out of bed and lurched toward her daughter's bedroom. It was empty, which made sense, considering that she had left her at Dad's house with a runaway boy. Leaning heavily against the doorframe, the room's emptiness tugged at her. She resisted for only a moment, then allowed herself to be pulled onto Lissy's bed, where she lay face-down on the pillow, breathing in the scent of her daughter's hair. She felt awkward and inadequate lying there spread-eagled, as though Lissy or someone else might walk in and find her there. Someone like Michael, Lissy's father.

"Ha!" she said. The syllable was muffled, but she knew what she meant, even if Michael, had he been there, would have had to say, "What?" Nor would he have been able to understand the next string of sounds that emanated from the pillow, but she thrust her middle finger toward the ceiling, so that anyone standing in the doorway would have gotten the gist.

She lay there long enough for the clock back in her own room to start singing. With a groan, she rolled onto her side and drew her knees up. Without Lissy there, she had no reason to turn the radio off, but from long habit she felt the pressure all the same—someone, somewhere, must be annoyed by it. She wondered when was the last time she had just listened to the radio for awhile. She didn't even know the song that was playing. How long had it been since she had allowed her own preferences to come before anyone else's?

She hated leaving Lissy with some strange boy—it was bad enough leaving her with her odd grandfather—but she had prayed for this, and she needed it. She would just have to trust that it would be okay.

Like it was okay for you?

Michael had been her own strange boy. He had taken his share of responsibility for their unintended consequence a whole decade before deciding it had all been a waste of time. The memory of his departure brought a coldness to her heart, and she stood up with no trace of morning grogginess. She walked back to her room and turned off the radio. She couldn't risk anything like Michael happening to Lissy. She'd just have to call in sick to work and go back to retrieve her.

She showered quickly—brusquely—berating herself for abandoning her daughter in the first place. At the breakfast table, she chewed her cereal with grim determination while she flipped open her Bible and devotional. She hadn't looked at them in weeks.

The bookmarks still opened to "The Command to Sacrifice Isaac," and her resolve faltered. What if God was testing her? What if he really wanted her to let go of Lissy for awhile, to trust him to provide the ram? Maybe God really wanted them to take a few weeks off from each other.

She shoved her cereal bowl away and put her head down on her arms. She wished the decision wasn't up to her. The decisions were always up to her, and she always chose in Lissy's favor, never in her own.

It's going to be okay, she decided. Her father knew from experience what could happen if you left a boy and a girl of a certain age unsupervised, and, while the boy was an unknown quantity, Lissy was strong and could take care of herself. She was too young to fall in love, as her mother had, or thought she had. Somehow or another it would be okay. It had to be.

"Dear Lord," she said, speaking into the crook of her elbow, "Please. *Please* keep Lissy safe. Give Dad the wisdom and vigilance he didn't have when I was young. Sorry if that sounds mean, but just give him wisdom and vigilance, and—I don't know—just let this weird boy turn out to be a good guy. And. Thank you for giving me this time off, for giving me a break when I needed it the most. Help me to trust you and . . . and leave it in your hands or whatever; you know what I mean. Amen."

She raised her head and checked to see if her new resolve would hold, decided it would, and stood up. She tossed her soggy cereal into the dispose-all and flipped the switch. She grimaced at what sounded like a robot vomiting, then rinsed the bowl and left it in the sink.

On her way back to her room to get dressed, she paused at Lissy's door.

"Enjoy our vacation, sweetie."

* * *

Calvin woke to an unfamiliar ceiling, cracked and stained in the bright morning sun. Bluejays and robins called to each other outside, and his pillow smelled fresh and stiff and old. *I could live here forever*, he thought, *if only they'd let me. If only Mr. Nowlen would let me stay and my father would let me go.*

He felt a jolt of fear at the thought of his father gearing up to look for him. Funny that he hadn't spent much time worrying about it when he was out in the woods. Now that he was safe inside, he imagined camouflage and shotguns, binoculars and knives. With an overwhelming sense of relief he remembered that he had started out wading through the river. His father was an experienced hunter, but even he would have a hard time picking up Calvin's trail. He ran through his movements the last few days, and recalled a haphazard and circuitous route that would confuse even Butchy. For the moment, he was safe.

For as long as he could, he prolonged the feeling of victory over his father. He lay with his hands behind his head, enjoying the smug grin stretching his lips. He thought of all the times his father had beaten him, both literally and figuratively, and his father's imagined frustration only served to increase his pleasure, until he made the mistake of picturing it too clearly and recalled the one time he had ever seen his father look scared.

He'd been six when Shawn, eight at the time, had pulled him away from the cartoon he was watching to say, "Go wake up Mom." He had heard Shawn trying to rouse her, so he knew there was some trick involved. If there was any blame to go around, Shawn always wanted his little brother to get the brunt of it. He couldn't recall if he'd actually done what his brother asked, because his next memory included Dad in the master bedroom, all three of them staring down at his mother's body. She was sprawled on the bed, her eyes open.

"She had a heart attack," their dad kept saying, his hands shaking as he picked up an empty pill bottle from the night stand. "Do you hear me?" he'd shouted at them. She was wearing her bathrobe, and her skin was yellow. "She had a weak heart. These," he shook the bottle in his fist, "are nothing. Forget you ever saw them." His voice was thick with emotion. "A heart attack." Calvin and his brother just stared at their mother's body while their father called an ambulance. Paramedics pulled a sheet over her face, and no one asked them any questions.

Calvin stared at Ed's ceiling, his eyes wide, his fists clenched, wondering why the thought of his mother's suicide never made him cry. At last, he got up, flinging the sheets off as though rejecting them, and went downstairs in search of breakfast.

. . .

From the corner of the Kitchen, Shep followed Son with his eyes. That he was moving around downstairs before Good or even Lissy arrived was suspect, but Shep would withhold judgment until the boy did something obviously wrong. If he tipped over the Garbage, he was going to get a sharp barking at. He shifted his ears when the boy took something out of the Fridge, but he wasn't clear that the Fridge was out of bounds for this one, as it would be for himself.

At last, another set of footsteps sounded on the stairs. Lissy entered the kitchen, and Shep set his tail in motion, thumping it against the floor emphatically. His ears shifted forward, but he did not yet rise. It was early yet, and there was no need to rush the bone-aching act of standing. Indeed, now that Lissy was here, Shep allowed himself to relax. She would bark if the boy caused any mischief. He snuffled at himself, a grim chuckle, knowing that she herself could spread Garbage all over the kitchen floor without Shep offering the least whine of disapproval. He closed his eyes and allowed her essence to wash through him. Her scent, though uniquely her own, carried with it undertones of Pumpkin and Kare Bear. He swallowed to think of all three of them back in the Kitchen. He had missed them so much.

A third set of footsteps on the stairs could only be Good. He stood up quickly, hoping to surprise the pain, but it came all the more sharply. With four paws underneath him, he stood stock still, waiting for the ache to recede, but then Good was in the kitchen, and Shep was walking toward him heedless of the pain, eager for that first pat on the head, the reassurance that he was still a favored member of the pack.

. . .

Calvin watched the old man place a hand on the mutt's head and say, "Good boy." *Must be nice to get a pat on the head just for existing*, he thought.

Mr. Nowlen proceeded to pour some food into the dog's bowl and take its water dish to the sink. The guy hadn't even poured himself a cup of coffee yet. He glanced at the cereal bowl before him and wondered if he'd be mad at him for taking food without asking. Just in case, he started eating faster, keeping an eye on Mr. Nowlen, who rinsed and refilled the water bowl and carried it back to the dog.

He drained the milk from the bowl while Mr. Nowlen made toast and, as quickly and quietly as he could, poured himself another bowl. Mr. Nowlen asked the girl if she had slept all right. Calvin couldn't hear the rest of what they were saying to each other because the crunching of cereal was too loud in his ears. By the time the man was sitting down at the table with his toast and jam, Calvin was slurping down the dregs of his third bowl of cereal. Mr. Nowlen looked at him coolly. *Here it comes*, Calvin thought. He tried to slow his breathing down, but he was panting; he had hardly given himself time to breathe. Nevertheless, he didn't drop his eyes.

"Hey, you ate all the cereal! Thanks a lot!"

"Now, Lissy, Calvin is our guest, and there should be more in the pantry. I see I've got a couple of early risers on my hands. I had planned on making eggs this morning. I still can, if you've got any room left."

Calvin stared at the old man, searching for the telltale signs of sarcasm, but he couldn't find any. He wanted to take him up on the offer, but his stomach was cramping. Instead of answering, he opened his mouth as wide as he could and tried to force a belch.

"I guess I'd better get to the store today. I forgot what vacuum cleaners growing boys can be."

"There's no more cereal in the pantry."

"Well, can I make you some eggs, darling?"

"I don't like eggs. Eggs are disgusting. They're gross."

"I see. How about oatmeal?"

"Eww."

"All right. How about toast? Would you like my toast?"

"Yeah, okay, sure."

Calvin watched Ed slide his plate toward his granddaughter, seemingly without resentment, then get up to make more. Apparently, you could get away with anything here.

* * *

The only reason Corwynn ever left her eaglets was to replenish their food. Alone and unprotected, they were constantly before her eyes, obscuring her vision, their vulnerable peeping drowning out all other sounds, even when she was miles away, talons clamped to the branch of a dead tree, glaring at the fish-concealing river that undulated like a languorous snake no matter how often she blinked to clear her vision.

Finally, she caught sight of a trout hanging inches from the surface directly below her. She bunched herself to dive, but at the same instant a young black bear loped out from under the trees on the river's far bank. As it plunged heedlessly into the water, Corwynn recoiled, flapping backwards involuntarily. After four or five wingbeats she recognized that she wasn't in any immediate danger and returned to the branch, her heart pounding. The trout, of course, was gone.

Anger flashed through her, and she pictured herself momentarily huge, able to descend with a shriek and plunge her talons into the flesh of the bear's back and clench his spine the way she was currently clutching the branch. With imagined strength she lifted the bear above the river and dropped it, dashing its bones against a rock. So strong was the vision that the branch on which she stood snapped in two and she found herself falling.

In her panic, she didn't know whether to fly or grip her perch more firmly. She was on the ground almost before she knew it, having managed to let go of the branch and open her wings only just in time. The bear was oblivious, rearing and splashing like a cub. She watched it wrestle with nothing, rolling around and around. Now it was on its belly, facing upstream, licking the water with deep affection. For some reason, the sight made her want to scream, so she did.

The bear looked up.

Peering around vaguely, its gaze went right past her. Seeing no cause for alarm, it returned to its slurping.

On a whim, she flew at the bear, but rather than attacking, she simply landed on its back. She did not grip, but balanced precariously. The bear paused only briefly, then accepted her presence without looking up. The fact that it did not shake her off—was not even startled but in fact was treating her as though she had a right to be there—lightened her heart. It seemed, indeed, to transform the entire world into a place in which she once again belonged, was welcome and safe. She reached down to rub the side of her beak into the bear's warm fur, lost her balance, and let herself fall gracelessly into the river. Normally, she hated getting wet, but now she immersed herself, spread her wings, and let the cold current seep through her feathers as it pushed her against the bear's flank. Seeing the bear begin to roll, she flipped sideways to stay out of its way. Together, they splashed and caroused till at last the bear decided it had had enough and waded toward the bank, where it heaved itself out of the water, shook great, arcing sprays from its fur, and lumbered back into the woods.

Corwynn watched its departure fondly, even as the current pulled her downstream. She angled herself toward a rock and somehow managed to clamber on top of it. She stretched her soggy wings and shook herself like the bear. She felt more awake than she had in weeks.

With more than the usual effort, she flapped her waterlogged wings until she regained the top of the same dead tree and waited for another fish to present itself. She had no doubt one would turn up soon.

* * *

While Lissy ate her toast, she considered the day ahead. One thing she remembered about spending time at Granddad's house: he only ever had two ideas about the proper way to spend a summer day. One was to work, the other was to fish. She knew of only one way to opt out of either. She waited till he was sitting down with a second round of toast to say, "Hey Grandpa, is my bike still in the shed?"

"Yuh. You'll need to oil the chain and pump up the tires, but I think she'll still roll."

"Thanks, Granddad." She got up, slid her second slice of toast into the trash, the dish into the sink, and pecked him on the cheek as she headed outside. "See you later, Cal." Shep was already at the door, so she held it open for him before running across the yard.

The bike in the shed was meant for a child, with a banana seat and plastic tassels dangling from the handlebars. She had wanted to bring her ten speed, but Mom said it wouldn't fit in the car. On the bright side, this one was still good for riding fast and popping wheelies. The WD-40 and air pump were right where she'd left them when she was ten or eleven.

The dirt road was bumpy, and she had to swerve to miss the bigger potholes, but the day was just getting warm, and the roads around here were endless and curvy. This was what was fun about Granddad's house: If she wanted to, she could ride all day.

A snake slithered out of the grass on the side of the road, and she swerved to miss it. For an instant her balance was in question, and a shudder went through her at the thought of falling on top of the snake, her face within range of its flickering tongue. The vision made her want to scream, and because she was alone—Grandpa's house reasonably far behind—she did. It felt good, so she screamed again. Then she started pedaling hard, to put some distance between herself and the squiggly little nightmare.

Out of breath, she let herself coast awhile, resisting the urge to check behind her to make sure the snake was out of sight and not somehow monstrously following her.

* * *

Shep trundled down the road in the direction Lissy had glided. He cast back and forth, sniffing the grass at each margin, but however low he dipped his nose, his eyes stayed fixed on the road ahead. He knew he hadn't been invited on this Walk, else Lissy would have waited for him, but perhaps she was just running off ahead like a puppy. Perhaps it was his responsibility to follow her to make sure she didn't get into trouble. It wasn't good for people to wander off by themselves. He himself still felt uneasy—even anxious, sometimes—when he was left alone.

When Lissy screamed, he broke into a trot. He knew from past experience that Lissy's screams did not always mean she was in danger; sometimes she was just having fun. But the second time she screamed he broke into a gallop that would have left a younger dog panting in his dust. She was farther away than he realized, however, and, as he put on a final burst of speed to catch up with her, she raised her haunches and picked up speed herself.

Shep stopped with difficulty, his paws sliding over the gritty ground, his entire body wracked with searing pain. He stood trembling, letting the pain wash over him, waiting for it to recede. He waited so long that a snake slithered—heedless of his presence—across the road just in front of him. He didn't have the energy even to bark at it. In the end, the pain overtook his patience, and with a whimper he turned and, limping, carried it back home.

· · ·

Corwynn felt lighter, which was strange considering that her feathers were still damp and a trout was clutched in her claws. She felt like she was floating, and though the pain of Kyron's rapine was undiminished, it was mingled for the first time with joy. She floated ever higher, until the day's scattered clouds were mostly below her, and her mountain was just a wrinkle in a land wrinkled like clutched fur. From here her aerie was a spicule, host to three mites. A tenderness welled in her breast to think of them so small and vulnerable in a broad, indifferent world.

A low whine, like the buzz of an insect, insinuated into her consciousness. She looked up, to where an enormous featherless bird flew so fast as to leave a wake of thin clouds. It was considerably higher than she, but at that speed it could easily outstrip her should it veer from its course and attack.

As the whine grew to a distant roar, Corwynn fixed her gaze on the three unguarded mites and tucked into a dive. She wished she were heavier now and that the air would get out of her way. She dared spare no backward glance, for a crooked neck would slow her further, but the roar was growing quickly while the circumference of her nest but only slowly expanded into branches and picked bones. The trout was slowing her descent, so she dropped it and tried to tuck her wings closer still.

When she was near enough to see her terror reflected in her eaglets' eyes, she assumed the monstrous bird must be right behind her, but then she realized she was coming in too fast and that she herself was the cause of their alarm. She flung wide her wings, pushing against the gale of her own descent, but though the strain stretched her tendons and the wind threatened to pull out her feathers, she barely slowed. She had no choice but to veer, lest her protective dive turn to ruin. Somersaulting past her thunderstruck offspring, she cartwheeled through foliage and hit the ground.

The monstrous bird was still visible, barely bigger than her nest had been from altitude, two long tracks of cloud behind it, stretching to the horizon. She flapped heavily to the treetop and flopped into her aerie. She wished her children to come to her, that she might press them beneath her breast, but they just stared at her stupidly from the surrounding branches. When had they learned how to leave the nest? When had they gotten so big?

• • •

Lissy had been pedaling for miles when she came to a side road that slipped down a steep hill. If she remembered correctly, there was a covered bridge at the bottom. She turned in a wide arc and coasted down the hill.

The bridge was old, with a sign on the far side describing its history. She rolled halfway across, rattling the thick, loose planks, then dismounted and sat on the railing while her heart and lungs slowly caught up with her.

Everything echoed, from the kicking of her heels against the old, wooden boards, to birdcalls, to the hollow sound of flowing water. She closed her eyes and released herself to listening. She didn't expect to linger, but the moments slipped in between her bones and made her their own. She became the bridge, the water, the breathless wind. She was a butterfly flitting through it all and dancing for sheer delight.

She is curled like a cat in a large and unknown woman's lap. The woman is talking to her, stroking her hair. At first Lissy can't understand the words, but then one phrase catches her attention and the rest comes clear:

"You are a sunflower. I am causing you to grow, straight and tall, a wonder to all who see you. Drink up my rains, draw nourishment from the earth, keep lifting your face to my light. A time is coming when you will be plucked from your lonely field, uprooted by rough hands. Do not be afraid, for I am with you, to sustain you through the darkness and cold of the approaching night. In time, I will replant you in a richer field, a valley teeming with sunflowers, a place where you shall have rest, a family, and a home. Therefore rejoice, for I am your salvation and your hope, and I will never leave you nor forsake you."

She opened her eyes, unsure if she had fallen asleep but feeling that a significant amount of time had passed. She tried to remember the dream she'd been having but couldn't recapture it. She remembered being held like a child. She remembered a woman's voice. She strained to hear again what the woman had been saying. With a smile a phrase came clear:

You are a sunflower.

18.

Calvin pushed the lawnmower back into the shed and leaned against the cool, dark wall inside, where the smell of oil and gasoline mingled with roasted grass from the mower's underbelly. Sweat cooled his forehead, his ears rang, and his body thrummed with the memory of noise and vibration. Without a task to occupy his mind, his stomach quickly grew heavy with dread.

In all likelihood, his father was waiting for him to return on his own once he got hungry enough, but his patience would evaporate once Calvin's absence made him angry. Were that to happen, his father's pursuit would be implacable. If anyone saw him here, or if Mr. Nowlen betrayed him...

A shadow blocked the door, and he nearly fell over backwards. "The lawn looks good," said Mr. Nowlen. "Thanks for doing it."

"Yeah, sure. Anything else I can do?"

"Oh, there's no end to work. There's weeds to hoe, brush to trim, firewood to gather. No hurry, though."

Calvin was already reaching for the hoe leaning against the wall by the door, but Mr. Nowlen was standing in the doorway and not moving out of his way. Calvin squinted at him, suspicious.

A long moment passed before the old man said, "First thing I want to say is you're welcome to stay as long as you care to. The second is, uh..." Mr. Nowlen put his hands in his pockets and looked down. When he looked up, it was only with his eyes. "I know your father, and, uh, I know about your ma." He took a deep breath and sighed through his nose. "Don't know the particulars of your family history—don't need to." He shook his head, working his mouth into odd contortions as if his words wished to come out in the wrong order. He eyed Calvin appraisingly and at last seemed to come to a conclusion. "I've decided I'm not going to call your dad. Don't know if that's the right, uh, call, but I've made it, and I'll not turn back on it." His eyes moved to one side as though sensing a problem with his decision, but he seemed to dismiss whatever it was and looked Calvin full in the face, his eyebrows up, inviting but not demanding a response.

Calvin nodded slowly, a gesture that made him feel like a grown up. He had no idea how to respond. Wild hope was surging within him, but he knew better than to trust it. He considered explaining why he had run away, about what really had happened to his mother, but the words didn't seem likely to come. "I don't want to be any trouble. I was just gonna, you know, live in the woods for awhile, live off the land." He realized he was still nodding and forced his head to stop. He couldn't quite meet Ed's eyes. "But then I found the owl, and, well, you know, it needed help and so . . ."

Mr. Nowlen was nodding seriously, as if mimicking him. "Well, you just make yourself at home." He reached out and clasped Calvin's shoulder, then turned and limped out of the shed.

Calvin spared a moment to wonder why the old man's touch sent tingles through his arm, then hurried to the rows of waist-high corn and tried to lose himself in hoeing.

• • •

From the bottom of this unfathomably immense nest, Æthel stared at a high hole that opened onto bright sky, blue and white. She had slept fitfully all day, the pain in her shoulder a constant, pulsing presence, but finally the ache was receding, and, despite the fullness of her belly, she wanted nothing more than to stretch out her wings and hunt. She strained against her bindings but was rewarded only with a fresh burst of ache. Occasionally, a finch crossed the sky from horizon to narrow horizon, and once she thought she glimpsed a robin.

She had seen such nests before—huge and squat and angular, abode of humans—but she had never been inside one before. The older, larger ones, typically of gray or red, were sometimes home to cousin owls, but she smelled no trace of kin. Alongside the present odors of bats and mice and squirrels, the older scents of dung and urine belonged (unless her nostrils deceived her) to cows.

She had never understood the bovine tendency to gather so close to human dwellings, but entering their nests voluntarily seemed absurd. She wondered if the cows she smelled had been captured, as she was—forced to dwell inside—but no, come to think of it, she had sometimes seen them, and other animals beside, entering and exiting such nests freely. She simply had never given the phenomenon a second thought.

She wondered about the motivations of her captors. Why both bind and feed her? She knew nothing of the human diet. They had implements that cut down trees and mowed down grasses, but she had never seen them eating what was felled. The giant beetle creatures, whose eyes shone like tiny full moons at night when they weren't sleeping unconcerned beside a human nest, regularly killed squirrels, chipmunks, skunks, raccoons—even birds, deer, and moose, though rarely owls—but left the carcasses uneaten. It seemed likely that they and their humans ate the cows and horses, sheep and chickens that surrounded certain of their larger nests, but their method of predation was unclear.

With mounting horror it occurred to her that their method likely involved gaining the trust of their prey by providing food and shelter, then killing and eating them only once their victims became fat and tender.

Ed unbuttoned his shirt and flapped it, then took it off and draped it over the back of a chair. His body was hoarding heat as though winter still lingered, and the stove was heating the kitchen intolerably. Also, kneading the bread had drawn a sweat. He pulled his undershirt out of his waistband and flapped that against his skin.

"Whooo. That's better," he said to Lissy, who was just walking in. "Your grandpa's having hot flashes."

Lissy smiled. "Well, no wonder," she said. "It's hotter than heck in here. Oooh! Are you making bread? Can I have some? I'm starving."

"Well, I shouldn't wonder. That's what comes of missing lunch. Where've you been all day?" He considered adding that he'd been worried, but he hadn't been—at least not until that very moment.

"Just out riding my bike," she said.

"Yeah? How far'd you go?"

"The covered bridge," she said, and though her tone was off-hand, he felt sure she intended him to be impressed, which, come to think of it, he was.

"No shit," he said.

"Yes, shit."

"Well, then you can have the first slice when it comes out of the oven."

"When will that be?"

"About twenty minutes."

"Then I'm gonna take a shower; I'm sweating like a pig."

"Okay, honey."

While Lissy clomped up the stairs, Ed turned his attention to peeling potatoes.

. . .

Calvin worked his way down a second row of carrots, and, though the sun was bright, his mind was on the darkness beneath the soil's surface, on the roots of the weeds he was ripping away, on the worms and centipedes the hoe was chopping into segments. The carrots themselves, lurid in the loamy womb of mother earth, ignorant of their ultimate fate in a pot of boiling water, feeling cared-for now, privileged to be the elect denizens of this corner of the garden... Leaning over, Calvin gripped green fronds and pulled, wanting to feel the satisfying tug and release of vegetable from soil, but the carrot came up with ridiculous ease, a tiny, orange blob not fit for a rabbit. He glanced guiltily toward the house as he used the hoe to dig an infant carrot's grave. As he dropped the greens down where roots belong, he tried to laugh at himself for feeling guilty over a murdered carrot, but the fear that he was being watched and judged wouldn't leave him. He filled in the hole and tamped it down, then hastily returned to hoeing, hoping to look as though he had never stopped.

He was into the peas when his stomach started rumbling. Leaning against the hoe, he glanced at the house. Mr. Nowlen hadn't shown him the snacks. At home there was always food about, and he knew how to slip into the kitchen to grab something and return to his room unnoticed—most of the time. Here he would be expected to ask politely and express gratitude for what was given. Letting the hoe fall to the ground, he set his jaw and walked toward the house.

At the edge of the garden he changed course, suddenly certain Mr. Nowlen was watching from the kitchen window. He searched for something he could be walking toward. The only thing nearby was the swing that hung from a tree branch, so he sauntered toward it with an air of purpose and sat down. He didn't put his full weight on it, but tried to look casual and at ease.

He wished he was home or still out in the woods. He hated feeling bound to some old man's generosity, dependent on his charity, and oppressed by his scrutiny. He wanted to be alone and independent—self-reliant. He slid his hands up the rope to shoulder level, felt awkward about it and slid them back down. He walked the swing backward but still couldn't surrender his weight. His hunger pangs mounting, he glanced furtively back at the house, wishing the old man would suddenly poke his head out the door and call him in for supper.

Suddenly he noticed the bicycle lying in the grass by the door. The knowledge that the girl was inside released him from the suspicion of being watched. The old man would surely be focused on his granddaughter. With a sigh of relief, he left the swing and headed for the door.

The first thing he noticed when he entered the kitchen was that Mr. Nowlen was standing over the sink in front of the window, peeling potatoes. The second was that Lissy was nowhere to be seen. He fought the urge to backpedal out the door. Fortunately, Mr. Nowlen wasn't looking up. Hardly knowing what he was doing, he lurched into the living room and sat down on the couch. Again, he found himself unwilling to relinquish his full weight but sat on the edge, his hands beneath his thighs.

Slowly, he noticed the smells of baking bread and cooking meat. His belly responded to them with longing. When the sound of peeling ceased, the faucet ran, and, when it stopped, a softer sound of running water continued. It took him a second to place the sound upstairs. In the same way his stomach responded to the smell of food, his groin reacted to the thought of Mr. Nowlen's granddaughter taking a shower.

He was struck by an overwhelming urge to walk upstairs, feigning a trip to his bedroom in the hopes of catching a glimpse of Lissy in a towel. Instead, he sat further back on the couch and pulled a throw pillow onto his lap, convinced that Mr. Nowlen would walk in any second.

When the shower stopped running, he convulsed. The desire to get closer almost overwhelmed his fear of getting caught. He leaned sideways slowly, to see if Mr. Nowlen still stood at the sink and stifled a gasp as the old man's face appeared in the doorway.

"What are your feelings toward beef stew, Calvin?"

"That's great!"

"It'll be ready in about half an hour. Feel free to turn on the TV if you're bored."

"Okay, thanks!"

Mr. Nowlen smiled and withdrew. Calvin reached for the remote and fumbled with the buttons until the news came on. He turned it up loud to drown out the sound of Lissy walking to her bedroom to get dressed.

• • •

Lissy wanted to go downstairs and watch TV, but she could hear the news blaring. She hated watching the news; it was just people talking, sitting behind desks or standing in disaster zones. She sat on the bed and rubbed the towel through her hair a little more. Dad used to watch the news, but she couldn't think of one time Mom had turned it on since he left. She wished there was a television upstairs, or even some good books, but there were just rows of the mystery novels Grandma used to read, their spines bowed inward, the titles illegible. She managed to pass five minutes daydreaming different ways to punish her mother—gaining privileges and designer clothes on the strength of maternal guilt over abandoning her—but daydreams weren't going to make weeks pass by any more quickly, so she took a deep breath and decided to make the most of it.

Downstairs, the strange boy was sitting on the couch, looking for all the world like he belonged there, watching the news at top volume. Granddad was puttering around in the kitchen making supper. She considered passing right through the living room and helping granddad, but before she reached the kitchen door she made an abrupt turn, walked to the couch and sat down. She would need to befriend the boy if her summer was to be at all bearable.

He kept his eyes fixed on the TV, but she suspected he was ignoring her more out of awkwardness than antipathy. Maybe he wasn't so entirely at home, yet, after all. She stared at his quarter profile. A slight movement in his eyes made her sure he was struggling with whether to turn and acknowledge her.

"Hey," she said.

It was almost funny watching him decide how to react. He was a moment-and-a-half too late to sell being startled. He straightened up and turned his head halfway, then turned it back, then finally shifted his whole body around and said, "Oh, um. Hey." He met her eyes only briefly, then dropped his gaze, noticed he was now staring at her chest and pushed his stare sideways.

Lissy smiled. Apparently she held the stronger hand in this card game. "Watcha watching?" she asked.

Calvin turned back to look at that stupid car commercial with the scared-looking eagle, then shook his head. "I don't know," he said. "The news, I think."

"Cool," she said. "Do you mind turning it down a little?" He looked down at the remote in his hand, and she watched him struggle with it for about fifteen seconds before taking it from him and turning the volume down to half. "That's better. So, what, you ran away from home?"

"What? Oh. Yeah," he said. "Yup."

"That's cool. I've thought about doing that before. You know, before the bitch threw me out." Her heart heaved at the meanness and unfairness of the word, but suddenly it seemed like the truth: how else to describe what Mom had done?

Calvin met her eyes again, and for a moment Lissy worried he'd see through her false bravado. Instead, he nodded.

"At least she cared enough to yell at your granddad about me. I don't think my dad even cares that I'm gone."

Ah, thought Lissy, *one-upmanship. This is definitely a game I can win.* "At least you've got a dad," she said, playing her high card first. "Mine left when I was ten."

"Ha," he said, and at first she assumed he didn't understand the game, but then he masterfully trumped her hand: "At least you've got a mom. Mine died last year."

"Holy shit," she said, then glanced at the kitchen and lowered her voice. "That sucks. What happened to her?"

"Heart attack."

Lissy reached for his hand and gave it a squeeze but let go when his expression changed. She debated ending the game, but she thought she had one more card that might help her maintain the power position.

"Yeah, well, at least she didn't abandon you, like my dad did. And my mom."

"Ha," he said again—that same humorless laugh. "Yeah." With that, he turned back to the TV.

Lissy couldn't figure out how she'd lost.

"Whatever," she said, and went to the kitchen to help Granddad.

· · ·

Kyron's mind was fixed on the shape of his mountain, and he was resolved to fly without food or rest until he attained it. Any thought of Corwynn or the eggs merely sapped his focus, so he put them out of his mind. Although the aerie itself was nothing to him—he had no emotional attachment to it—in his mind's eye it always contained, here and there, a downy feather from the breast of his love, piercing his heart, and so he excised the nest as well, and instead poured all his effort, all his pain and fear, all his yearning into reaching his mountain.

He had no way of knowing which was the right direction, and so he chose to fly against the wind, reasoning that the wind—that pervasive, inexplicable force—had blown him away from there, and so it was the wind he must battle to win his way home. He was not certain of his logic, but logic is not an eagle's strong suit. He had chosen a direction, and to alter course now was to admit defeat. The only thing he had to offer was his strength, so he chose the direction that would allow him to spend all of it in service to his quest. He would continue in this direction until the direction came to an end. Only then would he choose another.

For awhile, the constant flapping had hurt his wings, still weak from inactivity. They were shaped to embrace the wind, to hold the intangible—flapping was for ducks—but after awhile the pain dulled to an ache, then a numbness, and now, as the setting sun glared at him as though attempting to bar his way, he felt he could flap forever.

19.

Kyron sat in a tree, dazed and dozing, his resolve dissolving into doubt and defeat. He had not intended to let his feet touch down until he had regained his mountain, but the mountains had sunk into the ground. He had chosen the wrong direction—that much was clear—and yet, the direction had not yet ended, so what to do? Perhaps the mountains were only hiding, waiting for his faithfulness to be proven.

He needed a sign. He needed something to eat. He needed to sleep until...

He needed to shake his head, to clear it of confusion, but he was too tired. He knew his decision already: He jumped heavily back into the sky and continued on.

The mother of all rivers greeted Kyron with a spectacular sunset. The cyan sky was lacerated with orange, violet, red, yellow, and a single flash of green that glanced off the river's face and pierced his soul.

Welcome to the end of this direction, she said. *Take nourishment from my waters, for you have far yet to travel.*

The mother of all rivers was aswarm with eagles, wheeling and diving or sitting in the trees that lined her banks. She offered him a fish that had been left half-eaten on the ground. Almost he refused, remembering his vow, but *Eat*, said the river, and he understood that he had failed. He was farther from home than ever before, and his strength was utterly spent.

He couldn't be sure that the eagles around him were real and not merely made-up reflections of himself refracted through enormous, roiling waters. He alit beside the abandoned fish and, after a couple missed attempts, managed to connect beak with carcass and pull strips of flesh into his gullet. Nothing had ever tasted so delicious.

The other eagles accepted his presence in their midst as if he had always been there. They offered him their family and a rest from all his fruitless labors, but the mother of all rivers spoke louder.

Trust me, she said, *and I will bear you where I will.*

Kyron finished eating the fish, argued briefly and decisively with sleep, then unfurled his stiff and aching wings and jumped. A pain such as he had never known accompanied his torturous ascent. His wings, which had been numb and cold before, seemed now to be on fire. He persevered—because it was all he knew how to do—until at last the wind he had been fighting for days slipped underneath him and bore him up and back the way he had come. He let his wings relax and slowly their fire diminished as he wafted into the bosom of the night.

Fare thee well, my love, said the mother.

Summer, Part 2

21.

In her dream, she is always falling, alone in a starless night. Her wings, those intimate confidantes of the wind, are shattered, fluttering sickeningly as she falls supine—belly up like a poisoned fish. There is no fear of impact, for the gulf below is the infinite abyss of unassuageable loss.

When Corwynn pulled her head from under her wing, she was surprised to find the sun at the wrong horizon. She slept all the time now her eaglets had forsaken her.

Her daughter had been the first to leave, her wings strengthened by scorn, any fear overcome by resentment. Her eldest son followed, and her youngest, though he lingered many days, was the one to abandon her to Kyron's absence, a vertiginous void that stretched from their nest to the distant mountains like the wake of a swan.

She was finished. There was no one left to protect, no one to feed—not even herself—her strength was no longer required. She had accomplished the impossible—raised three eaglets by herself. Now let her cease from waking; let the sun bleach her bones, her vertebrae scatter; let the wind fill the sky with her feathers.

. . .

Mary sat down on the couch, picked up the phone and punched in some numbers. After several rings, Lissy's voice said, "Hello?"

"Hi, Lissy, just checking in again. How are you holding up? Are the boys treating you okay?"

"Yes, Mom."

"Good. I'm glad to hear it. Are you sick of fishing, yet?"

"No. We've only gone a few times, really."

"Oh. All right. Good. Well, just one more week, huh? Are you ready to come home?"

"Sure. I guess."

"Well, I can't *wait* to see you. The house just feels empty without you. Oh! I ran into Beth Anne at the library yesterday. She asked how you were and said to send you her love."

"Oh. Cool."

"Well. Enjoy your last week. It'll be over before you know it."

"..."

"Make good memories. I'll see you soon, hon, okay?"

"Okay."

"I love you."

"Love you, too."

"Okay. Goodbye."

"Goodbye."

Mary put the phone down and picked up the remote. The house rang with Lissy's absence. She had thought she would spend hours just drinking in her solitude along with the silence that accompanied it, contemplating life, loss, and purpose, but in reality she had spent most of the time watching TV. She caressed the power button with her thumb, vaguely aware that pressing it would hold at bay the guilt she still felt, but the idea of channel surfing through her final precious week alone was repulsive.

She set down the remote with exaggerated firmness and folded her hands in her lap. She closed her eyes. All she really needed was an hour or two of focused meditation to restore her sense of self.

Sixty seconds later, she decided all she *really* needed was a drink. The clock on the cable box said 7:28, she hadn't had dinner yet, and she hadn't been to Red's in years. The great thing about Red's, as Michael had always pointed out, was that it was well within stumbling distance. She stood up, grabbed her purse, and spent the next ninety minutes changing her clothes, fixing her hair, and putting on a little makeup. By 9:05, she was sipping a whiskey and soda, waiting for an unseen cook to fix her supper.

In spite of the disappointing fact that the bartender had not seen fit to card her, she felt giddy eating food at the bar. Almost she started giggling when her plate arrived; it seemed so wild and absurd. The bar was crowded for a weeknight, but there was an empty stool beside her, a group of guys talking loudly to one side and another group laughing boyishly on the other. She popped a french fry in her mouth and tried to suppress her grin by chewing. In the mirror behind the bar sat a lovely woman with shining eyes who would not stop smirking. They raised their glasses and drank each other's health.

She was on her third whiskey and soda when someone spoke into her ear, startling her. He was apologizing before she registered that he was asking if the seat beside her was taken.

"Yes! I mean: No! I mean, the seat's not . . . Feel free!" As the man sat down, she wiped her chin, wishing he had waited till she finished sipping her drink before asking. She glanced at him as covertly as possible. It was Mr. Haskins, Lissy's homeroom teacher from the year before. "Ted! Hi!" She wished she wasn't shouting everything.

"Mrs. Pea- Mary! How are you?"

"I'm good! How are you?"

"Great! I'm good, too. Really good. Fancy meeting you here!"

Mary laughed, then couldn't think of anything else to say. Fortunately, the bartender chose that moment to take Ted's order. She swallowed the rest of her drink and, when the bartender asked if she wanted another, said, "Sure!" even though she had been intending to ask for the check.

"So, how's Lissy?"

"Well, she's . . . my dad . . . she's living . . . she's staying . . . with her grandfather."

"Well, that sounds"

"For a few weeks."

"like fun. Where does her grand- . . . your dad, live?"

"Just about an hour and a half west of here."

"Ah. So not too far, then."

"No. She's just . . ." She wished the bartender would hurry up and bring their drinks already.

"It must be nice to have some time to yourself. A little alone time."

"It is." She smiled. "You have kind eyes."

"I'm sorry, what kind?"

"You have . . . Your eyes . . . I said . . . I said, 'You have kind eyes.'"

"Oh, thank you. You . . . too."

"Thank you!" she shouted.

"You're welcome!" said the bartender, equally as heartily.

"Cheers!" said Mary, at the same time that Ted said, "To being kid-free!"

The conversation went slightly more smoothly after that.

• • •

Lissy couldn't sleep. Granddad's house lacked air conditioning, and for the last two nights her bedroom had been unbearable. Even with the window open, she was sweaty and uncomfortable. With each passing minute she felt herself growing wider awake. At last she sat up, wiped the sweat from her face with the tangled sheets and decided to see if it was cooler downstairs.

It was, but not by much. She sat down on the couch, not bothering to turn on the light, and leaned forward with her elbows on her knees. In spite of her discomfort, the familiar smells of the room comforted her: the braided rug, on which she remembered playing Go Fish with Grandma; varnish from the rolltop desk and its chair; and countless, unidentifiable aromas accumulated over generations—the ghosts of her ancestry.

She listened to the house creak and pop, to the clock on the mantle tocking the minutes, until at last she slid to the floor. She was almost dozing when she was startled awake by the sliding click that presaged the chiming of an hour. It was five till two.

Sweat from her armpits dripped down her sides, and her butt was hot against the rug, as was her back against the couch. She wriggled down until she was lying on her side and pulled a cushion off the couch for her head. The clock struck two.

· · ·

Mary was only dimly aware of her clothes coming off, of Ted's hands groping, clutching, occasionally catching painfully in her hair. As if in a dream, she embraced him with her legs and accepted him into herself. Was she moaning or screaming? She arched her back, the pillow bunching uncomfortably beneath her neck. She surrendered to his rhythm as best she could until a question began forming in her mind, and she clasped his head in her hands, trying to see his face. His features were shifting, his eyes opening wide then half-closing, his mouth contorting—it was hard to tell. "Ted?" she said. "Ted?" At that moment, he went rigid, squeezed his eyes shut and looked up. Mary raised one eyebrow.

Slowly, like a calving ice shelf, he slid sideways, pulling out of her with a pop, and landed on his back beside her, gasping like a fish. Mary turned on her side and stared at his doubled profile, but as his breathing slowed it became apparent that he was already asleep. "Good night, Mr. Haskins," she said.

． ． ．

It was four when Lissy woke up, confused that the clock should still be chiming. There was drool between the corner of her mouth and the cushion. Lissy lifted herself halfway up, pushed the cushion back into its place on the couch, then dragged herself up and sat down on it. The room had finally cooled off, so she reached behind her and pulled the afghan around her shoulders. Her grandma had crocheted it the year before she died. There was one at home just like it, made the year Lissy was born.

She stared at Grandma's rocking chair, the one Granddad built when they first got married. Lissy always enjoyed sitting in it—thin, worn cushion and all. For now, though, she sat on the couch and imagined Grandma sitting there crocheting a blanket for her granddaughter's crib, looking up occasionally to smile at the phantom of that same granddaughter at thirteen. Lissy had always loved that smile, crooked teeth and all. It was sweet and simple and radiant, the way all grandmothers' smiles should be.

She stood up, crossed to the rocking chair and knelt before it. Looking into those glittering eyes, she smiled, placed her head in Grandma's lap and fell peacefully asleep.

． ． ．

Shep whumped his tail on the floor. Kare Bear had been so sick the last time he had seen her that he hadn't expected her ever to return. How Good had howled. Shep's own grief had been humbled by the depths of Good's pain. Would Shep keen so hopelessly if Good departed? The thought triggered a yawn, because the question was too big. Who knows how one will react to something impossible?

Shep drifted in and out of sleep, wanting to keep watch in case Kare Bear should enter the Kitchen, but she wasn't speaking or moving around, she was just... there, in the Livingroom where she belonged. Was she waiting for Good to greet her? Was she waiting for Shep to announce her arrival? Come to think of it, why hadn't he? Pain or no, he should be frisking like a puppy at her return, and barking like a TV set.

When he awoke again, he jerked up his head and sniffed. He could still smell her, but—no, he was mistaken—it wasn't Kare Bear at all, only Lissy, whose smell was really quite distinct, though she carried Kare Bear's scent like Good carried his Smokes. He must have been dreaming.

* * *

Mary could still smell the bar odors of grease and cigarettes, still feel the glide of her buzz, was just beginning to touch down on the landing strip of dry mouth and headache, but all she could hear was Mr. Haskin's insistent snore.

The time, according to the jittering glissade of the red LED, was 4:17.

The more she thought about the events of the evening, the more her body began to clench, starting with her crotch, settling in her jaw and ending in her fists, until she felt she might levitate above the bed like the possessed girl in that movie. *The Possessed*, was it? *The Dispossessed?* Something like that. Before long, she would probably be puking like her, too.

She swung her feet over the edge of the bed and sat up, grimacing as she tried to will her stomach into submission. She put her hand on her belly, as if on the head of an anxious dog, and slowly stood up.

Stepping into her slippers and shrugging on her light-blue flannel robe, she shuffled to the bathroom and softly closed the door. Absently, she switched on the piercing light and shuddering fan, then turned them both off with a wince. She lowered herself gingerly onto her knees and faced the toilet, uncertain which direction her stomach wanted to go. Only one question had the audacity to present itself to her consciousness:

Why, oh why didn't I stay home and watch TV?

22.

With the sun in his eyes as if to bar the way, Kyron worried he was flying in the wrong direction again. Ever since meeting the mother of all rivers, he had been haunted by the magnitude of his mistake, and he feared repeating it. But it was early morning, not sunset. He was famished and bone-weary as never before, despite the fact that he was no longer fighting the wind.

At first, after turning around, he had allowed himself to sleep and eat, feeling sure that the wind would bring him home within a day or two, but by now he had lost count of the sunrises that had arisen before him or to either side.

The wind had blown him hither and yon until he had been forced to conclude that it had forgotten him entirely and was simply gusting without purpose. The mountains had long-since returned, as if the ground were reaching up to touch him, but not one of them were his own, and he had ceased even trying to envision it. Only one image had the power any longer to keep him aloft—Corwynn, his love, whose eyes shone brighter than the sun.

· · ·

Ed walked downstairs in a bit of a daze. His dreams had featured Karen speaking earnestly, revealing secrets she had kept and explaining things that were happening now and were shortly to come. He didn't remember any of it, of course—he never put much stock in dreams, and certainly never wasted time trying to remember them—but the sense of Karen's presence was strong, and would likely cling to him all day. She was never far from his thoughts, but, after a dream like that, she seemed to be around every corner, or standing just behind him, or anyway somewhere comfortably close by.

He was in the kitchen filling the coffeemaker before he registered the body crumpled at the foot of Karen's chair. Curiosity gave way to concern as he set the coffeepot on the counter. Before he had re-traversed half the kitchen, a cold hand was squeezing his heart. Should he be running?

"Liss—" he croaked. It sounded more like a hiss. He tried to say her name again while simultaneously clearing his throat but accomplished neither. Suddenly there was phlegm in the space where his lungs met his throat and his breath caught, unable either to exit or enter. Choking or no, it was more important to reach Lissy's side than to breathe, so, even as he fell to the floor, he crawled to her, on his hands and knees, while his vision went black around the edges. It was no good: He had to breathe before he could help her. He pounded his chest with his fist and opened his mouth wide as if to vomit.

"Keh!" he said at last. It was enough to allow a thin stream of air to rasp into his lungs. He focused all his attention on not coughing until his lungs were filled, then expelled it as forcefully as he could.

"Granddad, are you okay? Oh my God!" cried Lissy, and with the speed of a striking snake she was on his back, her arms around his chest, fingers seeking his sternum, but she held back—*Good girl*—waiting to see if it was absolutely necessary, and—*Thank God*—knew enough about First Aid to understand that any breathing at all meant the Heimlich was a bad idea. Nevertheless, her reaction—proving that she was alive—released the tension from his bronchial tubes, and soon he was coughing normally. Lissy climbed off his back and stood over him, leaving one hand on his spine. "You *really* have to quit smoking," she said, and though she said it lightly, her voice trembled.

As soon as he could, he heaved himself onto the couch and pushed his back into it, still laboring to keep his tubes clear. Staring at the ceiling, he patted the couch beside him. When Lissy sat down, he put his arm around her shoulders. He couldn't form words—*What else is new?*—but he squeezed her close and hoped that his gratitude and love were communicated thereby—not to mention his admiration with her ability to rise from a sound sleep, grasp the situation accurately and act in the most helpful way possible.

She was looking up at him, and the concern on her face strongly recollected Karen. He raised one eyebrow. "Thanks for that," he said.

"I didn't really do anything," she said.

"Well, you did it right." With a wry smile, he gave her shoulders one more squeeze, then labored to his feet. "What can I get you for breakfast?" he asked, hoarsely.

"Just some toast," she said.

"One toast, coming right up."

* * *

Shep pushed himself to his feet and was surprised to find that he was shivering. It was taking all of his strength to remain standing. When Good came in a second time, Shep took a step toward him, only to have his hind quarters collapse. It was not so much the pain that made him whine as it was his helplessness. The fact that he could no longer walk toward Good was a loss too great to bear.

But this morning, Good came to him, knelt beside him, one hand stroking his neck, the other gently touching his rump. As the pain grew to a crescendo, Shep licked Good's face. For once the man did not pull back.

"Shep! Poor old pup. Seems like we're both breaking down this morning."

Shep gazed deep into Good's eyes and found there the strength to survive the moment. Then Good touched a sore spot and Shep yelped. Immediately he regretted it, but there was no taking it back. Good was standing up.

"Lay down, boy. Lay down."

Normally, Shep would have returned to his bed, but Good's tone was so gentle that Shep considered it obedience simply to slump to the floor.

"Good dog."

Shep laid his chin on his paws. Good always knew how to make him feel better.

. . .

Lissy raised her arms and arched her back. Her whole body was stiff and sore, and stretching toward the ceiling as she yawned felt utterly delicious, but, as soon as her arms went down, a weight of dread fell on the back of her neck, and she plopped heavily back onto the couch. What would she do if Grandpa had a real medical emergency while she was there? Strange Teenage Boy wasn't going to be much use. *God*, if he made a joke out of the whole thing, she'd punch him in the nostril, but then what? She no more knew how to give someone a Heimlich then she knew how to make a soufflé. She certainly didn't know CPR, and the idea of giving grandpa mouth-to-mouth was kind of gross. She didn't mind the occasional quick kiss, but his cigarette smell was really bad, and it might be too much for her, but then, just calling 911 and waiting wasn't a great option either. She hated herself for it but considered spending more time outside, so she'd stay ignorant of an emergency until it was too late to do anything. But no—that would be worse—walking in after several hours to find him sprawled on the kitchen floor, cold and stiff . . .

She shuddered and shook her head. What if he was lying there already? She pushed herself up off the couch and hurried to the kitchen. Grandpa was kneeling before Shep, who was lying on his stomach with his back legs sprawled at awkward angles.

"Oh nooooo!" she cried, rushing toward them and covering the last three feet sliding on her knees. "Shep, what's wrong with your legs?" Shep looked at her out of the corners of his eyes and licked his own nose. His tail brushed slowly across the floor. Granddad hadn't moved back when she arrived, so his face was absurdly close as she asked, "Is he okay?"

"Well, his hips don't seem to . . . I don't think he'll be tap-dancing any time soon." He smiled tightly, but his eyes were sad.

There was a moment of silence then, and although the possibility of death seemed all around her—or perhaps because of it—Lissy was overwhelmed with tenderness for the moment's closeness, its intimacy and connectedness. She and Granddad gazing into each other's eyes—sharing a mutual understanding of looming loss—made her feel like a grown up. She thought tears might be gathering in Grandpa's eyes.

He sighed and stood up, gasping through clenched teeth. In response, Shep shuddered and stood up as well, his back end trembling but holding steady. Lissy stood up, as well, and suddenly it all felt awkward.

"Were you just faking, Shep?" she said, bending over him and wagging her finger. "Did you just want some attention, huh?"

Shep shook himself as if he'd gotten slightly wet and took a few shaky steps toward grandpa, who reached down and rubbed underneath one ear.

"Good dog," he said, and Lissy heard pain and relief mixed together in his still-raspy voice. She decided then that she would do whatever was necessary to keep them both alive for as long as she stayed with them. She considered asking Mom if it could be longer than just the end of the week.

23.

Mary watched her computer screen turn black and start building sewer pipes—not for the first time that morning. She bumped the mouse and returned to staring at her work. She was struck again by how much she hated spreadsheets. Rows and columns—nothing out of place, everything neatly ordered—completely divorced from real life, but the roots and branches of business. She typed a random string of letters into one of the fields, but they only produced an error. There was nothing organic about them—they couldn't break the bounds of the grid, they didn't grow, never complained, changed nothing in the world but the configuration of a handful of computerized dots. She held the delete key down till the string of characters disappeared. As easily as that, the error was erased: No consequences; no regrets. An inverted metaphor for last night's fling.

. . .

Æthel's foot had been wrapped around the squeaking, squirming deer mouse since just before dawn, when it had heedlessly scurried right in front of her. Its fur was soft and warm and slid over bone and muscle in a manner that was oddly arousing. She wasn't hungry—the humans gave her cold, tender food every day, sometimes twice—and her bindings prevented her from lifting the mouse to her beak, but she yearned for the satisfaction of mammal in her throat. Once upon a time, deer mice had been her favorite prey. She should have been able to squeeze the mouse breathless, but her talons seemed listless and disinterested.

She couldn't figure out why this one had walked in front of her. It was as though it had wanted to be caught. Which was interesting. Was it unthinkable that her prey might experience a desire to be swallowed as visceral as her desire to swallow them? Her favorites tended to dwell in burrows; did they perhaps experience, whenever they returned home, a delicious sensation of being swallowed by the earth? Of course, she himself made her home in the maw of a tree. Did she have the same desire? She tried to imagine herself being eaten by some larger creature—a bear, perhaps, or a giant mouse. She let the image build itself within her mind, until suddenly it was so real that she shook herself in terror. Her bindings seemed to tighten, and she needed desperately to break free. Panic flared bright, threatening to overwhelm her consciousness, and she strained with all her might to spread her wings. To no avail. She forced herself to be still, to accept her constraints and remember that her situation had not changed from the last several days. Her question was answered: being swallowed was not a pleasant thought. The safety and familiarity of her hollow tree were dependent on her ability to depart at will.

She thought back on all the creatures she had killed to fill her belly—not ground dwellers only, but even birds and sometimes fish. She had eaten an owl once, much older than herself—caught him on the wing and ripped him to shreds. She remembered no remorse at the time, and yet how much greater must his real terror have been than her imagined fright?

She noticed with some surprise that she still clutched the deer mouse. It was no longer squirming, but as she stretched out her leg to look at it, it gazed back at her with black, blood-drop eyes, its whiskers barely twitching, its breathing quiet. She imagined opening her talons and letting the deer mouse drop. She imagined its relief and confusion. Would it scamper away, or would it pause? Might it return the favor and gnaw away her bindings?

Abruptly, the mouse resumed its squealing and struggled frantically. The insistent squeals threatened to bring back her own panic, and convinced her there could be no friendship here.

Nevertheless, she should let it go. She imagined it, but she didn't do it. Another pang had entered her heart—the loss of what was likely to be her last living meal. If only it would stop squeaking, so she could think things through, but its energy seemed boundless, and it had almost gotten one tiny claw over top of her talons. In frustration, she stomped it against the floor three times, and at last its cries dwindled to whistling gasps. She could feel its heart slowing against the base of her foot. At last, she dropped it, and it lay inert. Unable to bend, she let herself topple beside it. Side by side they lay, like two dead things, until at last she scooched her head forward and began to pull the mouse down the burrow—somewhat constricted with pity—of her throat, welcoming the deer mouse home.

. . .

When a junebug trundled past Corwynn's foot, she placed one talon on its back and stabbed it through. She hardly knew why. For whole days she would forget the reason for the emptiness gnawing at her heart. Only when she looked at the sky did she find herself searching for her mate, and so, over time, she had stopped looking up. When she lifted her foot, the beetle came with it, its feet waving in the air, one half of its carapace askew, revealing delicate wings. She regarded it carefully, noting its similarity to the dragon that attacked her nest.

It was waving its tiny antennae as though it, too, sought some answer to its predicament.

Abruptly, both halves of its carapace lifted, and its wings buzzed furiously. Remarkably, Corwynn's foot rose a bit higher, not of its own accord. For one mad instant, she imagined herself carried away by this black and oozing dynamo across leagues to the mammoth dragonfly's lair. But even that absurd hope was quelled by the certainty that she would find nothing there but Kyron's bones.

She scraped her talon sideways in the dirt, dislodging the bug, which crawled away, punctured and doomed. Without looking up, she took to the air, the film of bug goop cooling that one talon in the wind.

* * *

Lissy stabbed the earthworm twice with the barbed fishhook and dropped it in the brook. She was sitting on a mossy knoll that jutted over the stream like the crest of a wave, her heels kicking sand that trickled down into a deep, dark pool. The air was a little less oppressive, either because of the shaded water or because of the lateness of the hour, but the bugs were paying little attention to her bug spray. Calvin was a little ways downstream, straddling a dead tree that hung out over the water, barkless and sun-dappled, leaning against a branch that stuck straight up behind him. He looked like a painting of someone fishing, his pole held indifferently, his eyes half-closed. All he needed was a piece of hay sticking out of his mouth and a floppy hat pulled over his eyes.

Granddad was even farther down, standing in the middle of the river in his waders, steadily casting his line and reeling it in. He looked serious. So far, none of them had gotten a nibble.

She peered into the water, searching for some sign of life. She imagined a big, brown trout lurking in the roots just beneath her, happy to have a safe place to hide. She hoped it wouldn't notice the squirming worm floating above it. Fishing was boring, but actually having to deal with a living, thrashing fish with a hook stuck in its mouth would be ten times worse, so she lifted the hook out of the water.

She watched the worm writhe a couple of inches above the water's surface, dripping and trying to pull itself free. A guilty tension began to creep over her, and she kept watching Granddad out of the corner of her eye, ready to dunk the worm back in if he should glance over. Calvin seemed asleep.

As the minutes passed, the tension grew worse, which was silly—Granddad wouldn't care—but she felt like she was cheating, on account of some fish that probably wasn't even there. She dipped her pole to wet the worm and make it seem like she was really fishing, but the bobber still hung suspended a foot above the water. Her hands twitched, making the worm jump. It was getting hard to hold the rod at this angle. She wanted to slap herself for getting anxious on a fishing trip, of all things. Wasn't fishing supposed to be relaxing?

Suddenly the worm disappeared with a splash and a streak of silver. She screamed and dropped the rod in horror, putting her hands to her mouth. The rod fell in the brook—its reel spinning wildly—and floated downstream. She got to her feet and began to follow it, then stopped and looked at Calvin and Grandpa, both of whom were staring with their mouths open.

"I—I'm sorry," she called. She looked after the rod, feeling helpless. Granddad took a few steps and reached his hand into the water. When he pulled it out he was holding her line in the crook of one finger, letting the fish run, waiting for the rod to catch up. When it did, he pulled it out of the water and began to play the fish in.

He raised the rod straight up, then he let it slowly drop as he reeled the line in a little more. Then he lifted again, and so on, until the fish was close enough to be pulled clean out of the water, flapping and trembling. Calvin waded out to him with the net and together they walked it to the shore. She joined them reluctantly, not quite sure how to act.

Calvin held the fish while Granddad pulled the hook from its mouth.

"He's a whopper," said Granddad, seriously. "Our girl's been holding out on us, Calvin. We've got a master fisherman here. That's two, three pounds, easy. That's huge for this little brook. Nice going, Lissy. Way to show up the men."

While Grandpa took the rod back to the tacklebox, Calvin held the fish out toward her head-first. "This old fish didn't care about your worm; he wanted some of this." With that, he jabbed the fish toward her chest.

"Hey!" she yelped, jumping backwards. "Cut it out."

"Cut it out," mimicked Calvin.

Calvin had gotten a lot more comfortable around her the past few weeks, which she supposed was a good thing, but sometimes she longed for the days of his awkward shyness. Lissy glanced toward Granddad, who was bent over the tacklebox.

"Aw, what's the matter? Gonna cry to Pappy? Little fishy harassing you?"

"Grow up," said Lissy.

"Geez, it's a joke; don't get your panties twisted."

"Shut up," she said. Calvin made one more feint with the fish, but it started thrashing and almost got loose. "Whoa!" said Lissy, but Calvin managed to keep hold of its tail. Dangling it in front of his face, he looked at it cross-eyed, then thwacked it in the head with one knuckle. The fish went limp.

Grandpa came back with the creel. "We're eating fish tonight!" he said.

24.

Calvin was cleaning Lissy's fish at the sink while Mr. Nowlen puttered around making tartar sauce and slicing lemons. The princess herself was sitting at the table watching them, as though accidentally hooking a fish meant she'd done her part and could take it easy for the rest of the day. That kind of laziness would have been whupped out of her at his house, but as usual the old man indulged her.

Once the trout was butterflied and ready for the frying pan, Mr. Nowlen said, "What do you think, Lissy, are you willing to share a hunk of your catch with our friend Mr. Horns?"

Calvin opened his mouth to object, but, "Sure!" said Lissy.

"I know it might seem a bit extravagant, Calvin, but think of this as his farewell feast," said Mr. Nowlen.

"Aaaooohhh," whined Lissy, "Do we have to let him go?" Like she wanted to keep him as a pet.

"I'm afraid so. He's got places to be. His wing seems pretty much healed, and it's no kindness to keep him any longer. Calvin, pull a mouse-sized chunk off that trout, would you? Lissy, grab a pair of work gloves." Calvin scowled but did as he was told and followed them outside.

Although it was early yet, the porch light cast a pale glow on the grass. Mr. Nowlen was staring at the sky or perhaps lifting his nose to the wind. "Storm's coming," he said. Surprised, Calvin followed his gaze. The sky was cloudy, the wind fresh and gusting. He sniffed, trying to memorize the scent of oncoming storm; he'd need to be able to predict the weather if he was to survive in the wild, which he fully intended to get back to doing soon.

Lissy said, "Shouldn't we wait till after the storm to let him go?"

"He'll be fine," said Mr. Nowlen.

When they reached the barn door, the old man turned on his flashlight and cast its beam around. "Hello, Mr. Horns," he said, when the light picked out a burlap lump. "Lying down on the job, I see. How would you feel about a little farewell feast?"

They slowly filed into the barn, and Mr. Nowlen handed Calvin the flashlight, pulled on his gloves, and reached down to pick it up.

"There we are," he said.

Calvin held the fish near the owl's beak, but it turned its head away and closed its eyes. The stupid thing had never yet accepted food from him. "Fine. If you don't want it, I'll eat it myself," he said, and popped the fish in his mouth.

"Can I hold him?" said Lissy.

"Well, sure," said Mr. Nowlen. "Grab hold of its feet first. Get a good grip. There you go. Now, reach around and give it a hug. Yep." No matter how many times Lissy had held the owl before, the old man always had to give instructions. When Lissy had it, Mr. Nowlen unfastened the burlap. Immediately the owl slipped a wing out from under Lissy's arm and started to flap. "Hold it, Lissy! Don't let go!" Mr. Nowlen shouted, and Calvin was sure Lissy would panic and let go, but for some reason she was a lot steadier around birds than fish, and she managed to hold on until the owl settled down. "Good girl. Now hold it tight to your chest while I try to have a look at its wing." Moving slowly, Mr. Nowlen stretched out the wounded wing. "Keep the light on it, Calvin." He pulled the feathers back to look at the wound. "Mm," he said. "Mm-hmm." He folded the wing back and stroked its head.

"Is he okay?" said Lissy.

"He's fine. No sign of infection that I can see. I think we can let Mr. Horns go with a clean bill of health. Calvin, would you like to do the honors?"

"Sure," said Calvin.

Lissy leaned into Calvin to facilitate the exchange, and Calvin's body went all kinds of electric while he awkwardly grabbed hold of the bird. Once he had a good grip, Lissy stepped back and Calvin recovered somewhat, though he still felt the pressure of her breast on his arm. He walked outside, hugging the owl to his chest. While the others were still behind him, he kissed the top of its head and murmured, "Sorry I shot you, Mr. Horny." The owl surprised him by mewling softly, as if accepting his apology.

The sky was thick with dark clouds, but patches of blue were still visible near the horizon. He waited until Lissy and Mr. Nowlen were beside him, then ran forward and tossed the owl into the air. It caught its balance immediately, glided down almost to the ground, then flew away, its wingtips brushing the grass until it entered the woods and was gone.

"Goodbye!" said Lissy.

• • •

Æthel wasn't sure how she had escaped. One moment she had been surrounded by human limbs—grasped by dull talons—afraid for her life. The last one to clutch her placed its mouth upon her head. Preparing to be swallowed, Æthel barely had time to register that the mouth remained closed before she was suddenly airborne and flapping madly away. She was in the woods now, weaving through trees as though shaking off pursuit. At last she landed on a pine bough and spun her head to look behind. The forest was empty and silent but suffused with the menace of an approaching storm. Her escape would not be complete until she found her way home, but first she had to regain her bearings. She knew where her tree was in relation to the human nest, but she had no idea now where the human nest was; her careening flight had disoriented her.

As much as she hated flying near the river—where the rush of water overwhelmed every other sound—it was her only sure landmark, since clouds obscured the stars and mountain. She cocked her head and listened. It wasn't far, but instead of launching herself in that direction she sidled closer to the trunk of the pine, loath to leave its rooted stability.

Just then the wind picked up, and she realized that rain was imminent. With a rush of panic she pushed off from the trunk and flapped toward the river. It was farther away than she thought, and the downpour overtook her. Soon, the sound of the rain she had failed to outfly overwhelmed the sound of the water she was flying toward. Grimly, she persevered in roughly the same direction and hoped the river would find her.

. . .

When Ed slid Lissy's fish into the frying pan, he was surprised to discover that its missing chunk made him sad. It was as if the whole meal had somehow been designated a farewell feast: like the owl, his other two charges were about to fly the coop. Lissy would be returning to Mary within a week, and Calvin . . .

He couldn't understand how he had let so much time pass without telling anyone about Calvin. He had thought about it plenty of times but always put off actually doing anything. He had promised the boy not to call his father, assuming he had good reason to run away, but . . .

He had considered asking Calvin to explain his reasons and offering to accompany him to the police station if need be, but the timing had never seemed right, and he knew that if he waited much longer the weeks would start turning into months. He'd kept his ears open whenever he went into town but had heard no rumor of Calvin's disappearance. Frank must be keeping it quiet, though whether to give his son some space or to avoid any questions, Ed couldn't know. The matter hadn't seemed pressing before, but suddenly it loomed enormous. His chest filled with panic at the prospect of explaining to anyone else why he had waited so long to ask the boy questions.

He wished he had a close friend he could discuss the matter with, but since Karen died, he had been keeping to himself. There had been a flurry of visits in the weeks following her death, of course, but . . .

What he needed was a priest, or a lawyer—someone he could be sure would keep the matter confidential—but he hated lawyers on principle and hadn't been to church since Karen's funeral. Still, he had liked the pastor who had done her service. He seemed like a trustworthy sort, quiet and grounded.

He looked out the rain-streaked window. There was no telling how long the storm might last, but it was easy to imagine how long excuses could pile up. *Better wetness now than regretness later*, he thought.

Yep. As soon as supper was over, he'd pay a visit to Pastor Massey. Get some advice. He poked the fish with a spatula and decided it would probably cook faster if he turned the burner on.

· · ·

Calvin sat on the edge of Mr. Nowlen's guest bed and wondered what the fuck he was doing. Here he was, feeling trapped inside, when what he wanted— what he'd wanted all along—was to be free. The premise that had sent him out of his bedroom window so many weeks ago—that nothing matters and therefore he could do anything, anything at all—had thus far brought him right back where he started.

He was deeply embarrassed by his actions this afternoon—so childish—and he was so turned on by his brush with Lissy that a part of him was still pointing straight up.

It sucked, because he always held everything in, and when he didn't, it spewed out all wrong. He had been acting like he was 11, when in reality he was 17. He could have sex with her if he wanted to. He could . . .

I could have sex with her if I wanted to.

He imagined stepping up behind her and cupping her breasts. Would she lean into him and hum, or would she drive an elbow into his gut and spin away from him, screaming for her grandfather? As much as he tried to imagine the former, his fantasy Lissy kept morphing into the latter, until he was convinced she would never accept his advances.

⁂

Mary looked out the window and wished for a fireplace and someone to snuggle with. She dismissed the idea of calling Ted before it fully formed. She'd be happy enough never to see him again, and he'd likely not be content with snuggling.

Lissy was a good snuggler, and Dad's house had a fireplace. Dad's house had two fireplaces. She searched her heart for the will to drive through the storm and ask him to build a fire in front of which she and Lissy could snuggle. *Hmm. Tempting.* But Dad would be hard to convince. He wouldn't understand the sense in building a fire in the middle of July, thunderstorm or no.

She remembered when Mom used to complain of being cold. "Put a sweater on," was Dad's invariable reply. "I'm wearing a sweater," Mom would say. They'd been repeating the same exchange right up until the day Mom died. Mary pulled the afghan off the back of the couch—the one Mom had crocheted for Lissy's crib—and wrapped it around her shoulders. Thunder crashed, rattling the windows. She wished Lissy were already home.

25.

At first, Lissy assumed Calvin didn't know that his foot was touching hers beneath the table. She was trying to think of a clever response, something like, "Keep your feet to yourself, sailor" or "Tap your *own* toes, Tucker," but she thought she could do better. Except that now he was rubbing her ankle with his big toe, and she didn't know what to do. She searched his face for some sign that he was teasing, but his gaze never left his plate as he steadily shoveled food into his mouth. For a moment she wondered if she was imagining things, but then the pressure of his toe caused a wave of sensation to sweep through her body. It was the same sensation she used to get when Dad made a game of lightly stroking the hairs on her arm. She looked at Grandpa, who was equally absorbed in his dinner, and tucked her feet beneath her chair.

Soon something touched her knee and slid down the side of her calf, then crossed her shin and went up the other side. Was he flirting with her? The thought was equal parts revolting and exciting. Imagine entering freshman year already dating a senior! But wasn't he supposed to smile slyly, even if he wasn't looking at her? She almost snorted with laughter at the realization that it was Shep under the table, begging for food. But nope, Shep was lying by the stove, his eyes following Granddad's fork. She lifted her own fork to her mouth, but there was no food on it. Was she turned on or creeped out? How would her girlfriends react if she were to whisper this to them on the playground? Would they squeal and blush or gag and retch?

She pushed her tongue against the empty fork that was still in her mouth, as if the sharp pain might clarify her thoughts. Calvin and Grandpa kept eating. Calvin's foot circled endlessly, tirelessly, and Lissy's body was shaking in time with her heart. She ate some green beans, chewing only when she remembered to close her jaws.

She decided to wait until she and Granddad were washing dishes to tell him what Calvin was doing. She tried to think how she could phrase it so that he would be equally likely to nudge her with his elbow and laugh it off or kick him out of the house. She tried to ignore the foot as it moved to her other knee, circling there, cold on her bare leg. The amount of food in front of Granddad was unchanging and eternal.

But at last he was tilting his plate, so the heel of his fork could scrape the mashed potato from the slight recess near the edge. She pushed her chair away from the table so quickly that Calvin's foot hit the floor with a thump, and Granddad at last looked up, but without curiosity. He stood up while she was dumping dishes in the sink, and said, "Well, I best get a move on if I want to get back before bedtime. You kids behave yourselves now." Lissy picked up a glass, thinking to drop it as a signal that something was wrong, but she couldn't let go.

"Where are you going, Grandpa?" she said, dismayed by the casual tone of her voice.

"Visiting a friend," he said, already reaching for his raincoat and the cane he hardly used anymore. "I should be back in a couple of hours or so."

She paused for effect, trying to think of something—anything—to make him stay, but all she could manage was, "Bye."

"Goodbye, honey," he said, and walked out the door.

Lightning flashed, blinding Æthel for a moment, so that—when the crack of thunder made her flinch—she collided with a thick branch.

Standing on the ground, trying to shake the wet from her feathers, she realized she was lost. It was raining too hard; the trees were too close together—she needed space. She leaped upward and flapped wildly through the canopy, leaves and twigs brushing her wings until she was rising above the forest, cold and wet but free.

She continued rising, fighting the wind and rain that threatened to wash her from the sky. If she could only see the stars, she could orient himself. At the least, she'd be above this pitiless downpour. Soon she was within dark cloud, and she redoubled her efforts, rising swiftly, with nothing but gravity to indicate which direction to flap against.

The cloud seemed endless and endlessly turbulent. Though her wings were heavy, stiff, and wreathed with pain from long disuse, she shut her eyes and forced herself higher, hoping to lose herself in pain and struggle—to leave behind the loneliness of the massive human nest—to know nothing but wind and wings' strength.

Abruptly, the wind shifted, and she opened her eyes. The cloud seemed less dark, the air warmer and rising; with her wings spread wide she could ascend without flapping. Tremendous cracks of thunder and lightning exploded around her, but she felt removed from her body, an observer merely, and in no immediate danger.

Her dispassion lasted until she noticed her breath coming short. She flapped once and felt ice crackle amongst her feathers. With surging panic, she beat her wings at the thin air. Moments later a frigid blast sent her tumbling, pushing her out of the cloud at last and into a sea of stars. The glory took her breath, which had already grown rapid and shallow. The stars bloomed into fuzzy, particolored flowers and then she began to fall, though whether down, up, or sideways, she couldn't tell.

* * *

Lissy washed the dishes by herself, keeping an eye on her reflection in the window in case Calvin tried to sneak up behind her. Each flash of lightning startled her. When she finished, she turned to the table, expecting him to be sitting there still, but he was gone.

She wished she knew where he was. The TV wasn't on, so he probably had gone up to his room. She thought about calling Mom, maybe asking her to come pick her up, but it would take at least an hour and a half for her to get out here. She considered going outside until Granddad got home—maybe take Shep for a walk. At night. In the rain. "Stop it," she whispered. A thump startled her, and she turned to see Shep wagging his tail against the floor. "Goodbye, Shep," she said. "I mean, 'Good boy.' I mean, 'Good night.'" She patted him on the head and walked toward the stairs on the sides of her shoes, trying to keep the floorboards from creaking. She tiptoed past Calvin's closed door and locked her own behind her.

Immediately, she felt foolish. Maybe she should knock on his door and ask him what he meant by playing footsie with her. Maybe she should make out with him a little. She and Beth Ann had had to listen to Jenna and Heather about their first kisses. She wasn't a little girl anymore. With Grandpa gone, now was her big chance. She leaned against the door and took a deep breath.

"Eww," she said, suddenly. "Not with Calvin. God."

She changed into sweats, turned out the light and crawled into bed, not yet thoroughly convinced she had decided against anything, but . . . "Eww."

When her closet door creaked open, she screamed. Downstairs, Shep woofed in response, and she yelled, "Shepherd! Here boy! Come here, Shep!" as a figure loomed in the darkness.

* * *

Kyron was cold, weak, and lost, but Corwynn's eyes still filled his vision, urging him beyond despair. A massive stormcloud loomed before him, crackling with electricity. He ought to fly around it, but the peril seemed unreal. The fact that he was about to be savaged by wind and drenched by freezing rain seemed strange, inevitable, and not terribly important. Almost he didn't notice the clump of debris hurtling toward him.

For a moment it looked like an owl, tumbling crazily on the wings of some strange draft, and he assumed he had slipped into a nightmare. Then he saw that it really was a great horned owl with half-closed eyes and wings akimbo, not even bothering to flap. He snatched the raptor deftly, amazed by the neatness of it. Then the turbulence caught him and jolted him wide awake. Together they tumbled, and for a moment their eyes met. The owl wore the strangest expression, as though of recognition, but Kyron had never in his life been this close to an owl before.

She was dead weight in Kyron's talons, and every instinct insisted he open those talons and release their burden, but, little though he knew of owls, he was certain they were ill-equipped for thunderstorms at this altitude. Though Corwynn's eyes still beckoned, he was unwilling to sacrifice this storm-wracked bird to his hopeless, lovelorn quest, so he resolved to return the owl to the forest where she belonged.

Lightning flashed directly below them, and the thunder galvanized him: The only way through the maelstrom was to become as lightning himself: he willed his weary wings to renew their strength and shot through the clouds with a yell.

. . .

"What are you—Stop! OOOOWWW! Cut it out. Please. Just stop it, okay? Pleeeease, oh my God, please!" Tears streamed into Lissy's ears, one of her breasts was on the wrong side of her bra, and the shadowy figure on top of her was pulling her underwear down. With its other hand it grabbed a handful of hair and pulled her hard into the pillow. It was Calvin—who else?—but she couldn't see his face. She thrashed like her trout, clawing at the face, the chest, the arms, but the figure was too strong. "SHEPHERD!" she screamed, though she hardly knew why. She could hear the useless dog thumping up the stairs, its claws scraping wood.

When she heard the clink and zip of Calvin's pants coming undone, she tried to fuse her legs together, but he lifted them both and dropped his full weight on top of them, jamming her knees into her ribs. "Come on," he said. "It'll be fun." A flash of lightning revealed his face, his mouth smiling, his eyes glinting, followed almost immediately by a boom that shook the house. For a moment she considered trying to believe him. He let go of her hair and she had time to wonder if he was going to kiss her before his hand grabbed her neck and squeezed. With a grunt he thrust himself inside her.

She tried to gasp but couldn't get air into her lungs. She scrabbled at his hand, but his fingers were like tree roots. It felt as if he were pulling her guts out through her vagina. Overwhelmed by terror, pain, and asphyxiation, she rejected the moment, got out of bed, and walked to the window. Outside, in the bright sunlight, a field of sunflowers stretched to the horizon, waving slowly in the gentle breeze.

Behind her were sounds of grunting and gurglings, but the view was so beautiful and inviting that it brooked no distractions. She opened the window, breathed in the smell, and thought how nice it would be if she could just float gently down and skim through the tops of the nodding flowers.

Somewhere close by, a dog was whining, scratching at the door, begging to be let in.

Poor fella.

* * *

Corwynn dozed fitfully in the midst of the downpour. The thunder held no more terror for her, but the soaking rain was puddling in the aerie, making her feel like a duck. She pushed her head further beneath her wing, seeking deeper sleep.

When lightning crashed directly overhead, she flinched so hard it hurt. Her wings half-raised, she cast a baleful eye toward the clouds and was bewildered to see an owl descending like a second bolt. Even in the dim stormlight, she recognized the owl she had once dumped in a river. In her confusion, she almost failed to notice its second set of wings.

* * *

As soon as Calvin came inside of Lissy, his lust turned to shame and disgust—like a match that's been snuffed, smelling of sulfur. He pulled out, let go of her throat and stood up. Looking down at her, he considered apologizing, but she was pretending to be asleep. As he pulled his pants up, lightning flashed again, its thunder muted and delayed, the storm moving off at last. It was eerie:

while he was fucking her, the thunder and lightning had seemed constant, joining Shep's barking like shouts from God. He backed into the door, startling himself, then turned and fumbled with the skeleton key until it turned. Shep pushed through and waddled straight toward Lissy. Calvin didn't wait to see how she responded, but went to his room and started packing. He wanted to be as far away as possible before Mr. Nowlen returned.

His groin felt awful, like it was wrapped in a shit-filled diaper.

. . .

Kyron clutched the edge of the aerie and teetered, drenched and dripping, awaiting some sign from his mate that he was welcome home. Corwynn was staring at the owl he had dropped in the nest, and Kyron was staring at her, drinking in her bedraggled beauty.

She placed one foot on the owl's back, a gesture so graceful it curled his tail feathers. She looked up, and the force of her gaze made him yelp. He gripped and regripped the edge, buzzing with anticipation. He would wait forever so long as she never drove him away.

The owl between them convulsed, and Corwynn winced. Slowly, he divined her hesitation: she thought he intended the owl as an offering she should eat. He might have laughed, if eagles laughed. Instead, he put one of his own feet on the owl's heaving back and raised his beak toward the storm clouds. She cocked her head. He cocked his head in the same direction and willed her to understand him. Just as he was beginning to believe she never would, she launched herself at him, and they tumbled out of the nest. Branches struck his back and head, disorienting him, but his wings and talons scrambled blindly until he was flying upward, following his love's bright form into the clouds, all weariness forgotten.

He overtook her in the dark and cold and wet, and grasped her warm, soft body. Together they plummeted, grappling, and then he was inside her, and all around her, and she was all around him. They fell as one, the raindrops no longer pelting but caressing as the ground pulled rain and eagles alike to its bosom. Cheek to cheek they dropped until there was little space left to fall through. They parted, spread their wings and landed in sopping bracken, only to return to their grappling, their every point of contact a lightning strike of intimacy and a thunderclap of joy.

26.

Ed got home later than he had intended. Pastor Massey, despite his quiet demeanor and concise sermons, had a way of keeping a conversation going longer than any other human would consider desirable. Predictably enough, he had prayed with him about Calvin but hadn't offered any concrete, practical advice. Ed hung up his coat and listened half-consciously for Shep's tail to thump against the floor. When he didn't hear it, he frowned. "You awake, old friend?" He turned on the overhead fluorescent and looked around. Seeing that Shep wasn't there relieved him somewhat; he'd been half-afraid the old dog might have fallen asleep for good.

Perhaps one of the kids went out walking and took Shep for protection against the fierce, wild creatures they might imagine prowled the forest. But then, it was still drizzling, so that didn't make much sense, either. He switched off the light and limped upstairs. He was still concerned about Shep, but he was also tired, and long experience told him there were perfectly good explanations for most things out of the ordinary.

At the top of the stairs he noticed Lissy's door was open. That, too, was unusual. He poked his head in and saw the lump of Lissy's body curled away from him. He reached for the door to close it when he heard a single, familiar-sounding thump, followed by a low whine. "Well, *there* you are, boy," he said quietly. "What are you doing up here?" For some reason, Ed sniffed the air. He shook his head and went to his room, leaving Lissy's door open in case Shep wanted to leave. He was about to pull off his shirt, when it occurred to him that it had been a long time since Shep had attempted the stairs. Again he was troubled. Somehow things weren't as they should be tonight.

He considered waking Lissy and asking if anything strange had happened while he was gone. He had no sooner dismissed the idea then he found himself walking back to her room and turning on the light. Shep watched him as he reached over and nudged Lissy's shoulder. "Lissy," he called, in a whispered falsetto. "Lissy?" She didn't respond. More puzzled than alarmed, he put two fingers to her neck, feeling for a pulse. She shrank from his touch, pulling her shoulder up to shield her neck. Ed straightened, frowning. Shep whined again. "Did you get into a fight with Calvin?" he asked.

Lissy curled up tighter, like a spider that's been poked, and, with a low moan, said, "No," in a way that didn't seem to be a response to his question. Ed's heart went cold.

"Calvin." His heart was thumping as he walked to Calvin's room and pushed open the door. The bed was stripped bare, the sheets on the floor. The room was empty, not only of Calvin but of all his things. "Oh dear God," said Ed, his hand bunching his undershirt above his heart. "Oh dear God. Lissy!" He went back to her room and sat down on the edge of the bed, shaking her shoulder. Tears were rising, threatening to fall. "Lissy!" he said again, his voice quavering.

At last she rolled over and clutched him, burying her face in his belly. He put his arms around her as best he could and sobbed. "Oh dear God, no. Oh no." He was rocking back and forth, shaking, tears falling into Lissy's hair, her sweet face. Shep stood up and put his head on Ed's knee, staring at Lissy "Shep," he said. "Oh, Shep." Shep rolled his head sideways and licked Lissy's hair.

"Oh, no."

● ● ●

Mary hung up the phone and stared out the window. Dad said he had made a fire, and that he and Lissy were watching it. She felt a surge of hatred against him, talking so calmly and gently about how her worst fears had come true—and he had taken the time to light a fire before calling her. As if a fire would help. She got up to make herself a cup of tea, then remembered that she had to go, had to—wouldn't that be any mother's first instinct?—run to protect her child, to comfort—to avenge, if nothing else. She grabbed her purse and ran out to the car, her mind racing. She remembered Lissy's baptism, her first communion—hadn't it been enough? *Michael should be here. If he hadn't left, this never would have happened.* She wiped tears from her face as if they were gnats. *She's thirteen, for God's sake, she doesn't even. There's been a mistake. She probably just got angry and started making wild accusations.*

Oh God—what if she's pregnant?

Mary had no idea, when she pulled up next to her father's house, how she had managed to get there. She had no memory of the road, of other cars or of any landmarks. She shut the door too slowly, and it didn't fully latch. She opened and closed it again more firmly, took a deep breath, and knew that if she stopped to take another she might never go inside, so she strode up the front steps as if confident of her competence as a mother when she knew she was no such thing and never had been since the day she squeezed Lissy from her loins and let the doctors whisk her away.

It was a wonderful fire. Better than she had imagined, big and blazing. Lissy was sitting in Dad's lap, sucking her thumb. *That happens sometimes,* she thought. *They regress.*

"Lissy," she said, and was not surprised that her daughter didn't look up. She knelt beside the chair and put her hand behind Lissy's head. Still no response. "Why isn't the ambulance here, yet?"

Dad lifted his face towards her. Salt crystals trailed down his cheek, and his eyes struggled to focus. "Ambulance? What?" He was holding Lissy as if she were a newborn made of antique porcelain.

She was grateful—actually grateful—that he hadn't called an ambulance, because it gave her an opportunity to shift the blame that weighed so heavily upon her.

"*Jesus*, Dad," she said. "This is serious, okay? Do you get that? Do you understand what just happened? Cuddling by the fire isn't actually helping anything, okay? *Jesus*." She listened to her voice rise in pitch and realized she wasn't actually doing anything, either.

"Lissy, honey, it's time to go." She tugged her daughter's arm. Lissy shook her head, exactly as she had when she was two years old.

"Go on, Lissy, go with your mama," said Ed, half lifting her out of his lap. At last she turned and held her arms up to Mary, who hoped she could get to the car without dropping her.

"Call the hospital, Dad, and let them know we're on our way. Can you do that much?"

"Sure."

He looked utterly lost. Mary searched her mind for something else to say, but nothing came. She hurried to the car. By the time she was buckling Lissy into the front seat, her arms felt like logs. She leaned against the hood of the car and felt her bottom lip begin to spasm. *Nope*, she said to herself, *there will be time for that later. Right now you need to be strong.* She stood up and forced her mind to be still. She walked to the driver's side door and got in.

Before she started the car, she turned deliberately to Lissy. "Everything's going to be okay," she said, and reached out and patted her knee. Lissy stared straight ahead like a mannequin. Mary turned the key and took a deep breath. "Everything's going to be okay," she repeated.

27.

Lissy just wanted to go home. People kept touching her, asking her questions. Every touch, gesture, and word felt like a slap. She just wanted to sit on the couch with Grandpa and watch the fire, not sit on this paper-covered vinyl cushion, under glaring fluorescent lights, being touched and prodded and interrogated by gentle, well-meaning strangers.

"I want to go home," she said, hoarsely, for the eleventh time. She was counting to see how many times it would take. For future reference. "Can I go home, now?" Twelve.

"I know this is hard," said a woman dressed in white, "but it's important that"

Lissy didn't listen to the rest.

28.

Corwynn kept watch all night, the moon casting as many stars in the fallen raindrops as sparkled up above. Kyron was sleeping beside her, returned from the dead. What victory he had wrested from the dragon's maw she would never know, nor from what darkness he had wrested the owl she had dumped in the river. Had he plucked them both from the depths of the sea?

An owl and an eagle asleep in an aerie, and she alone bore witness. Would he recognize their children when they visited, or would he chase them away as intruders? Let the morning decide; tonight was for gratitude and awe.

. . .

Mary wanted to explode. All her concern, all her guilt, all her fear—had been displaced with rage during their stay in the hospital. Now they were back in the car—finally on their way back home—and all Mary wanted to do was to scream at Dad for leaving Lissy alone with that shit-headed monster for one second.

But she had to get Lissy home. She had to keep herself together, for Lissy's sake. She had to be gentle and caring and motherly for Lissy, who recoiled whenever she tried to touch her, pressing into the door like a mouse shying away from a boa constrictor in a cage.

Her imagination failed to provide sufficient things she'd like to do to the boy. Unspeakable things. Things that would take a long time to finish.

As if she was hearing the news for the first time, she remembered what the doctor confirmed the boy had done, and then she was shaking the steering wheel as though her hands were around his throat. She wanted to honk the horn and scream, but she looked at Lissy, who hadn't reacted, and reminded herself that she had to keep it together. She had to get them safely home, get Lissy safely in bed. . . .

Except that it was too late to get Lissy safely anywhere.

It did not seem possible that the drive would ever end, and yet, after several years, it did. Lissy got out of the car as soon as it came to a stop, and Mary followed her. At the door, Lissy jiggled the handle, pushed and pulled to no avail but showed no signs of stopping. Mary watched her daughter's efforts as though she herself were hypnotized. Then she remembered locking the door, something she almost never did, a gesture as futile as anything else she'd done lately. "Ridiculous," she muttered. She nudged Lissy gently aside and unlocked the door, then let her daughter enter first.

She barely had time to hang her purse on its hook before Lissy was heading upstairs saying, in her painfully raspy voice, "I just want to be left alone, okay, Mom?"

Although Lissy's footsteps were like hammer blows to Mary's heart, she steadfastly refused to explode.

* * *

Ed pulled the shotgun from its place behind the living room door, checked the breech, loaded two shells and whistled for Shep. Having failed to involve the police when Calvin first arrived, he would not involve them now. He listened to

Shep's tapping claws exit Lissy's room and come to a halt at the top of the stairs. He laid the gun on the table and headed toward him. When he reached the foot of the stairs, he looked up at Shep looking down. Knowing the dog would waddle down on his own if he didn't move, Ed climbed up toward him. Shep would need to make it downstairs in one piece if he was going to be of any use. As he ascended, thinking about the nature of the help he needed, he realized he had another reason to go upstairs. Shep followed him into Calvin's room, where Ed picked up the bundle of tossed bedsheets and pushed them into Shep's muzzle. "Find him, Shep," he said. "Find Calvin."

• • •

Shep recoiled from the sheets, confused. Good's gesture recalled a time before he had learned not to piddle inside, but he was not to blame for soiling Son's bedding. Nevertheless, Good's eyes were implacable, so Shep leaned into the fabric without breaking eye contact.

"Find Calvin," Good repeated, and it finally dawned on him what he was asking. He knew Son's scent well enough; he backed away and headed for the stairs, but stopped again at the top step. His hips were trembling already. He wagged his tail, took two steps in place with his front paws, then glanced at Good and back at the stairs. He reached down to sniff the top step. He was ready; he could do this. He reached one paw down, gingerly, gingerly . . .

And then strong arms grasped his chest, and he was lifted up. His back against Good's breastbone and his legs dangling, he rolled his head around, trying to lick Good's face, but the jolt of the first step down returned his attention to the stairs.

He felt like a human child, like the most beloved member of the pack. His hindquarters bounced with each stair and each huff of Good's breath, and an odd heat seeped into his bones.

When Good set him down, his flanks no longer trembled. In fact, he felt no pain at all. While Good tromped away, Shep shook himself vigorously, starting with his nose and ending with his tail. It was no illusion—all his pain was gone.

Somberly, Shep walked into the Kitchen, where Good was already at the door, the Shotgun (*krakoom!*) in the crook of his foreleg and something silver in his paw that was painfully bright at one end. He hurried to his water bowl to slurp some cool wet, then turned and trotted through the open door and into the sodden night.

A few paces out he put his nose to the wet grass. There was no mistaking the direction Son had fled. He did his best to bay (being more of a woofer), and cantered toward the woods, trusting Good to follow.

* * *

Æthel regained consciousness reluctantly, fearing what she might return to. Was she lying shattered on the ground, in a pool of blood and rainwater, the pain beyond her register? Was she back in the cavernous human nest, her storm-ravaged freedom a dream? The breeze convinced her that the latter could not be the case, so she opened her eyes to inspect the damage, and instead was greeted by eagles.

She closed her eyes again, returning to dark ignorance. When they opened again, it was singular—one eagle only—fast asleep. She felt as weak as a chick, but unbroken, and from the position of the eagle's body, she knew that her companion was equally helpless. It was as if they were nest-mates, awaiting their mother's return.

Cautiously, she tested her muscles. Her legs flexed with ease; her neck turned; her mouth opened. Her wings ached from exertion but seemed otherwise whole. She was stiff, and still in the grip of much-needed sleep, but upon reflection she felt remarkably hale.

The realization sent a thrill through her torso, and she pushed herself upright. She spread her wings—scattering water—puffed out her breast and greeted the free and open darkness with a hoot of elation.

• • •

Corwynn strangled the milk snake as she flew, its writhing contortions acting as a rudder on her flight. She had found it beside a human nesting site, where patches of light dispelled the darkness. It was slow to give up the ghost—distances were harder to judge at night, and she hadn't caught it clean—but by the time she gained the aerie, the snake was limp in her claws, and she twined it beside her lover—but out of reach of the possibly greedy owl, strange intruder, staring with humongous eyes—who would be allowed to eat only after her lover was full.

Kyron had not moved since their ecstatic coupling. His dim form looked and smelled half dead. She tore the snake as she would for a hatchling, and offered him a trailing strip. She drew it back and forth across his beak, to wake him and trigger his hunger.

• • •

Æthel watched with wonder as the eagle who had rescued her in the woods tore a strip of flesh from the corpse of a snake and patiently drew it back and forth across the beak of her unresponsive mate—the eagle who had rescued her from the sky. She felt like an intruder on an intimate moment, but her wonderment arose from the fact that her presence was accepted. It had been so long since she had had company, captors notwithstanding. Now, it seemed, she had friends.

The prone eagle twitched, but something was wrong—he was not merely asleep. His breathing was shallow, and although his eyes occasionally fluttered, they never opened. What had he been doing in the midst of that storm?

On an impulse, Æthel bent toward the eagle's beak. The snake flesh was pulled away—no doubt her first savior assumed she was trying to snatch it, but that was not her intent. She hooked her beak beneath the mate's and lifted. Up close she could smell death on him, but he was not yet dead. The neck swiveled, but that was not enough. She could feel the eagle's eyes upon her, and she knew that if she made one wrong move she would be attacked. She had no doubt who would come out the worse in a fight. So she moved slowly, and gently pried open the unconscious beak and pointed it skyward.

Satisfied with her work, she stepped back and dipped her head at the standing eagle, who regarded her with an inscrutable eye, then stepped forward and dropped the snake flesh into the open maw. Part of it was draped over the edge of his mouth, so she took the end and folded it over, where it lay in the back of his throat.

Æthel could feel pleading in the eyes that looked up at her, and for a moment, she was overwhelmed by a wave of helplessness. She closed her eyes until the feeling passed and a memory visited her of the gentle human who had helped her swallow. First she closed the eagle's mouth and then, under the she-eagle's wary eye, she bent lower and stroked the eagle's throat with her beak. Her face was too broad to manage the feat effectively, so she stepped back and dipped her head again.

Hesitantly, the she-eagle leaned over her mate, twisted her head, and drew the top of her long beak down the feathered neck. Æthel swallowed heavily, the tenderness flooding her mouth with moisture.

It happened so suddenly she almost missed it. The eagle's throat convulsed, and his mate shook her head in surprise. She looked at Æthel as if to confirm what she had seen, then she turned to the snake and removed another strip of flesh.

Calvin emerged from the endless patch of scrub oak with relief. The widely spaced pines and waving ferns before him promised much easier travel. The only reason he had entered the stand to begin with was to shake off pursuit, since he had spent the first few hours of his flight traveling in a straight line. Within the scrub oak, he had circled, backtracked and made random sharp turns, going uphill and down until he was sure neither man nor beast would be able to follow him. But the scrub oak had not ended when his need of it did. No matter which direction he turned, sharp, stiff branches had snagged his hair and clothing and scratched his hands. In the mazy, moon-dappled darkness, every sound had been amplified, and he had felt vulnerable and exposed, but at the approach of dawn his fears had dwindled with the sense that he would see someone coming before they saw him. Now that he was through the clawing branches, he was free to pursue his earlier course and get as high up and as far away from Mr. Nowlen as possible.

Heh. Up, up and away, he thought.

"NO!" cried Lissy, and Calvin almost turned around.

"Stop," said Calvin. He was standing on the side of a mountain, all alone.

"SHEPHERD!"

He was in her bedroom, and Lissy's neck was warm. Her head was whipping back and forth, her hands scratching at his face.

He picked at his cheek with his fingernail, which came away with dried flecks of blood. He hadn't even noticed. "I didn't...." Whatever he was going to say felt hollow, like a lie. He had. He *had* meant to. "I'm sor—"

"Don't you *dare* say you're sorry," screamed Lissy's voice in his head. Or was it his mother's? Did it matter?

Did it?

. . .

Shep's quarry was so easy to follow that Good could have tracked Son by himself. Even now, when the spoor led into a thicket too dense for Good to enter, the whiffs he had been following were suddenly overwhelmed by the scent on the breeze. He looked back at Good—still plodding sturdily along behind him—then bounded forward the last few lengths. There was Son, looking in the wrong direction, completely unaware that he had been found.

For a moment he heard Lissy crying out in fear and pain, and doubt darkened his mind. Had Son been the source of Lissy's dread last night? He had been the one to open the door, and that had been an act of kindness, but one of the smells in her room had been blood. Shep took a hesitant step forward.

When he nosed his hand, the boy recoiled and kicked out with his foot, grazing Shep's muzzle, then fell over and scrambled backward. It was as though Son didn't recognize him.

"Oh God. Shep. Oh shit," said Son, who was now lying down, his eyes darting back and forth like a housefly.

Shep cocked his head.

"Here, boy," said Son. "Come over here, you big, dumb dog."

Shep didn't really understand that last part, but he'd been around long enough to recognize the sound of trickery. He backed up a few paces and shouted for Good to come quick.

* * *

For the first hour, Ed's mindset had been grim. He had been mentally prepared to walk for days—to pursue Calvin into the next state if necessary. He hadn't known exactly what he would do when he caught up with him, but he figured the shotgun would cover pretty much any contingency.

But as Shep had led him straight up the steepest parts of the mountain, his resolve had begun to falter, and since hour two it had taken every ounce of willpower to hike ten minutes before taking five, and he'd had to admit that he was not actually capable of catching up with a 17-year-old boy. "Well," he had said to himself then, and he repeated it now, "That's no reason to stop trying. What else am I going to do with the rest of my life?"

The thought still had the power to rouse a spark of his fury—enough to get him moving again—but he was careful to restrain it, wishing it to explode only when he set eyes on . . .

"All right, Shep, I'm coming."

He stood up slowly, checking his balance, and retrieved the shotgun that was leaning against a tree. Once more he began to climb. By now the pain was almost enjoyable. He hadn't pushed himself so hard in years, and the endorphins were pumping around like whiskey and soda in his veins. Maybe Shep felt the same way.

"No time for chasing squirrels, Shep; we've got a—Oh, it's you."

Calvin lay sprawled on the ground, as though Shep had pushed him, and the expression on his face was pure terror. He was staring into Ed's eyes and didn't even seem to have noticed the shotgun yet.

"Good dog," Ed said, not taking his eyes from the boy. Shep wagged his tail and galumphed to his side.

He opened the breech and checked the ammo. Birdshot. Why had he loaded it with birdshot? *Because I wasn't paying attention*, he thought, ruefully. It probably wouldn't kill him, but it would sure hurt like hell. He waited a beat before looking back at Calvin, whose eyes had grown even wider. He was backing away like a crab, his mouth open but making no sound. Ed closed the breech but wasn't yet ready to take aim.

He watched Calvin slam his head into a rock, wince, push himself upright against it, shift his eyes back and forth and slowly conclude that there was nowhere to run.

A cold shiver ran through Ed's heart. He could picture himself crossing the short distance between them, shoving the barrel under Calvin's chin and pulling the trigger. *That* would probably kill him. He looked down at the gun, drew a deep breath, looked back into Calvin's terrified eyes, narrowed his own, and took one step forward.

A dark stain spread across the groin of Calvin's pants, obvious even against the camo pattern.

Ed grinned, more for effect than pleasure. He had never in his life been so close to murder. He had never imagined it might feel so . . . satisfying.

Calvin's eyes and nose were running, his mouth contorted, but his gaze remained locked on Ed's. He began to raise his hands, fingers splayed, then slowly returned them to his side, where they hung limply. Finally, he bowed his head, inadvertently protecting the flesh beneath his chin.

Ed glared at him for a long time, but in the end, he had to acknowledge that the boy had won the performance aspect of their encounter. He nodded, disappointed. Had the boy tried to run, Ed was quite certain he would have shot him in the back. Had the boy said he was sorry, he was reasonably sure he would have clubbed him to death with the shotgun's stock. But this—piss, tears, submission—this earned him the right to live, at least for another minute.

"Get up," he said, gruffly.

Calvin got up and, without conversation, started walking downhill. Shep followed him, and Ed—accepting, provisionally, Calvin's assumption—followed Shep.

* * *

Lissy felt like a brass statue of herself, sunk deep in her mattress and covered in blankets as though she'd been put in storage. Where had she heard the saying, "Ridden hard and put away wet"? She shied from the image—it was too apt.

There was a hand on her foot.

Had she been dreaming that? It seemed unlikely, and yet—yes—she had been dreaming about a hand on her foot. As she probed the memory of her dream, it seemed that two hands had occupied her sleep for hours—one at her throat and one at her foot.

The slightest movement of her leg would suffice to confirm or deny the sensation, but in truth she didn't really care. She and the mattress and sheets were one, and the hand on her foot, if it was there at all, seemed harmless.

She could hear her heartbeat through the bedsprings. It was strong and slow and steady. She listened to its two-note melody until she was almost asleep again. Then her leg twitched.

There was a hand on her foot.

More curious than afraid, she pulled her head out from under its tangle of blankets and into the light of day. Mom was kneeling at the foot of the bed, mouth open, eyes closed, head leaning on the shoulder of the arm that tunneled beneath the covers and terminated at Lissy's ankle. Overwhelmed with pity, she jackknifed her torso and placed her own hands on her mother's head and face.

The moment before her mother's eyes opened lasted forever, but then Mom was reaching for her face as well, and trying to get up, and groaning because she was stiff. Lissy wanted nothing more than to curl up in her lap, but it took an awkwardly long time for Mom to situate herself into a sitting position and open her arms. Lissy's mouth was stretched in a frown, and her eyes welled with tears, but at last she was snuggled and embraced and all was right for a moment. She was crying, and laughing at her tears, and her mother was, too, and then they were quiet, and she could almost forget why they were there. But then, when she was almost asleep again, she heard herself asking, "Does it always hurt like that?"

Mom drew a sharp breath, gripped her tighter, and pushed her mouth into Lissy's hair. The warmth of her breath eased the ache in her scalp. *Kiss the boo-boo*, she thought. At last Mom cleared her throat. "Sometimes," she murmured. "Sometimes it does, but not always. Sometimes it's wonderful. It's just—you have to be ready."

Yesterday, she thought, *this conversation would have grossed me the fuck out.* "That's good," she said. "'Cause it still kind of hurts, actually."

"Oh, baby," Mom said, and it was more like a sob.

Lissy sighed. Her mother was not really equipped to deal with this sort of thing.

. . .

Corwynn straddled Kyron's back, rocking from side to side to cover more of him, rising and falling with his breath as if she were floating on a lake. It was an awkward position, but she wanted to impart some of her warmth and life into his struggling body. The owl had flown away after the feeding, but she caught glimpses of her from time to time, silently circling the aerie as though keeping watch.

She concentrated on Kyron's heartbeat, on pouring her life into his. She wished she had more to give—that she hadn't let so much of her vitality leak out in despair. No matter. What she had she would give—to the final drop.

• • •

Mary wished she could sit there forever, stroking Lissy's hair in the half-light of her daughter's curtained bedroom, but her leg was sore where Lissy's head had been pressing against it for the past hour.

"Are you awake, sweetie?" she whispered.

"Yeah. Is your leg hurting? It keeps twitching." Lissy sat up, and looked at Mary with genuine concern in her eyes.

"Oh God, Lissy—you're sympathizing with me—now I know we're in trouble."

Lissy snorted. "Nice, Mom."

"That's more like it."

Lissy laughed, and Mary laughed with her, and for almost half a minute she felt like everything was going to be okay—but then she heard the false note in Lissy's laughter—that she was trying to convince her mother and/or herself that everything was going to be okay—so Mary stopped laughing and put her arms around her and pulled her close, but Lissy wouldn't stop, and Mary wondered if it had ever been natural laughter, or whether Lissy wasn't simply hysterical, and her helplessness—Lissy's and Mary's both—caused panic to rise in Mary's chest.

Whatever control she had over her own emotions was about to slip. She needed a second to collect herself—to gather the resources to stay strong. She extricated herself as gently as she could and stood up. "It's okay, sweetie. Let me get you a glass of water. Okay?"

"No! Don't leave me!"

She said it exactly the way she would have when she was five, and Mary could see it coming—implacable, unavoidable—a tidal wave of emotion that would sweep them both away. She had barely a second to escape it—to pull herself and Lissy clear. She grabbed Lissy's shoulders and shook her. "Stop it!" she commanded. "Just stop it, Lissy. Right now!"

Lissy stared at Mary with wide eyes, and for half a moment Mary dared think her tactic had worked, but then Lissy's face went slack, her eyes half-closed. She pulled away from Mary's hands, curled up in the corner of her bed and put her thumb in her mouth.

"Oh God, I'm so sorry, Lissy, I'm *so* sorry! It's okay, baby. It's okay. It's . . . oh God, *oh God*." And then she simply collapsed on the floor, put her arms around her knees and started keening, hearing the same little-girl tone in her own voice but impotent to do anything about it. She was hoping Lissy would empathize again, but she was clearly beyond that, now—beyond reach, beyond comfort—and so Mary wept while her daughter withdrew into herself, and there seemed no hope that either would ever stop.

• • •

Calvin shook his leg mid step, trying in vain to get the fabric of his pants to separate from his skin. His penis was uncomfortably positioned and getting pinched with every step, but he felt too self-conscious to adjust it with Mr. Nowlen right behind him. The only good thing about his discomfort was that it distracted him from the scenarios playing out in his mind. In one of them, he would run away from the excruciatingly slow old man and his friendly dog. Shep seemed spryer than usual, but the shotgun would prove faster than any of them, so Calvin would have to get that away from him. He was pretty sure he was stronger than Mr. Nowlen, but he wasn't sure he was ready to bet his life on that belief. And then again, what was Mr. Nowlen going to do once they got back to the house? Call the cops?

Damn it, he should have been more careful, not left evidence. He'd be convicted for sure, but that realization only spun his mind into a series of prison scenarios, where he was lifting weights in the yard, bulking up, beating the shit out of anyone who tried to fuck with him. Except people in prisons moved in gangs, and if there were enough of them he might be overpowered. But then again, there was a possibility that the shotgun was just for the wedding. He'd be Mr. Nowlen's son-in-law, and things could go on the way they'd been. He and Lissy would take over the master bedroom, and Mr. Nowlen would move into one of the guest rooms. It might take Lissy awhile to forgive him, but he'd show her what a good guy he was, really. And plus—he'd get to have sex with her whenever he liked. He risked a glance behind him. Mr. Nowlen was focused on stepping down from a small boulder, so Calvin took the opportunity to readjust his penis.

It was too bad the old man would never trust him again, never make him another sandwich, never call him "son" again, but there remained the simple fact—almost comforting—that Mr. Nowlen and Shep had come after him, just like his father and Butchy had not. He glanced back again. The shotgun was leaning against the rock so that Mr. Nowlen could use both hands to lower himself.

Now would be the perfect time to grab the gun and take off running.

. . .

Æthel heard the dog coming long before it was close enough to pose a threat, but she was astounded to discover that it was the same one that had growled and snuffled at her when the smelly human had delivered her to its enormous nest. She had newfound respect for the dog's tracking abilities. Not every sniffer could follow a bird in flight, especially a flight as wild and unpredictable as hers had been.

And yet, having found her, they continued on as though she wasn't there. The dog was in the lead, the one who had retrieved her from the river followed after, and the old one with the soft talons was bringing up the rear. The only one missing was the smallest—the one who had figured out how to feed an unresponsive bird.

She knew these humans to be capable of inscrutable choices, so, despite her weariness and the brightness of the day, she decided to keep an eye on them as long as they were near her saviors' aerie. Silently, she fell in line, swooping from branch to branch behind them.

30.

Ed was regretting the shotgun.

They were resting again—and even though they were taking an easier route down the mountain, his hip was whining like a puppy in a thunderstorm—Calvin on a rock, himself on a fallen tree, while Shep restlessly investigated the woods.

He had not set out to retrieve Calvin; he had set out to kill him. He hadn't admitted that to himself before now, but it was true, and the fact that he had accepted Calvin's humiliation in exchange for his life was rankling him. He didn't know exactly what the boy had done to Lissy—his mind shied away from imagining it like a horse from a rattlesnake—nevertheless, her face kept swimming up in his mind's eye. She had been hurt. Not mortally, maybe, but the boy had taken something from her that could not be returned. Whether it was her virginity or her innocence or her belief in the goodness of people—or something else that he didn't have a name for—there was no doubt in his mind that this—this sniveling, grotesque excuse for a human being—had violated...

Just thinking about the word *rape* made him want to point his gun at Calvin's testicles and squeeze the trigger. The fact that he continued to fail to do so made him want to lift the barrel to his own chin. He felt certain that he was dishonoring Lissy's trauma by placidly walking along behind her attacker, the boy who had betrayed them both. He coughed, spat out what came up and lit another cigarette.

He knew better than to demand an eye for an eye. He knew better than to judge without knowing the facts. He knew better than to sit here in stony silence—or he ought to. And the worst thing about the shotgun was that it could be taken away from him in a moment. If he wanted the truth, now was the time to ask, while he still had the upper hand. Not certain he could handle the *what*, he gritted his teeth and asked, "Why'd you do it?"

He could almost see the adult and the child at war within Calvin, but the wary way Calvin was eyeing the shotgun told him he had not misjudged the crime.

"I . . . I dunno," he said.

"You can do better than that," Ed growled. "I don't care if it takes all day. Dig deep."

. . .

Shep ranged back and forth between the downhill slope and Good, who was resting again and talking to Son. Shep was scouting and exploring and bounding through the underbrush. He felt heavier and slower than he had when they set out, but stronger, too, and there was still no pain in his hips.

In this tiny meadow were butterflies, midges, and a big spider hanging in an open space between two branches of a bush, the new sun glancing off each drop of water on its web. Whenever Shep noticed his own wetness, he gave his whole body a shake, but the water was everywhere, so it didn't do much good.

Here he smelled a deer that had spent the night in this matted grass. Here was her scat. Here he smelled another dog that had crossed this meadow yesterday. He couldn't be certain, but he remembered smelling a similar dog on Son the first time they'd met.

He jogged back up the hill, stopped in front of Son, and woofed, inviting him to come check out the scent himself, but Son made no move to follow. He took a few steps in the right direction, then turned and woofed again. Still, Son didn't move, too interested in something on the ground to pay attention.

"Go on, Shep," said Ed, with more growl than usual. "Git."

Git was a serious word, so Shep obeyed. He supposed the smell could wait until the pack was ready to move again. In the meantime, he decided to continue uphill to make sure they weren't being followed.

Not far away he saw an owl like the one from the Barn sitting in a tree. He barked and looked back, but *Git* still hung heavy in the air, so, absent instruction, he sniffed the ground—keeping his eyes on the bird—and cautiously approached.

Suddenly, the owl shifted form, growing twice as big and hissing. Startled, Shep ran, first toward Good, then, on second thought, away. As soon as he dared, he skidded to a stop and looked back. He saw no sign of the owl, so he woofed. Instantly, something swooped to the ground not far from where he stood. It was a huge, round creature with the owl's wide eyes and a ghastly hissing, and he turned again and ran, dodging trees, bounding over bushes, zigzagging and occasionally rolling himself over. Quick glances behind assured him the owl was still in pursuit, and he barked for pure joy.

Oh, was there anything finer in all the world than chasing and being chased?

• • •

Lissy was sucking Calvin's cock, perfectly well aware that it was also her thumb. She wanted to bite down, draw blood, sever tendons, spit his wiener out in the dirt, and wear it on a chain around her neck like a trophy. Instead she put her hand between her legs, and he was licking her there until she squeezed her legs around his neck. As his face turned purple, she pushed her thumbs through his eyes. She rolled over, twisting his neck a hundred and eighty degrees, and sat on his back, bouncing up and down as if playing horsey. Though her thumbs were still wet with his aqueous humor, his eyes were whole again, but rolling up into his head. Then his body untwisted, throwing her off, and he was on top of her, pinning her hands to the bedsheets, his eyes ablaze with fury, their noses almost touching. A drop of sweat from his eyebrow dropped onto hers.

Slowly his eyes softened. "Do you want to do it again?" he asked.

She wavered, then nodded, and he kissed her, and kept on kissing her as they removed each other's clothing, and she wrapped her legs around his torso as he entered her. She gasped—her nondaydreaming fingers doing his work for him—as pleasure commingled with pain.

When it was over, he kissed her again and asked her tenderly if she would marry him. "Yes," she said, without hesitation.

She walked down the aisle with Granddad and lifted her chin as she passed her mother in the front row. She kissed her grandfather on the cheek before stepping up beside Calvin, smiling sweetly, and turning to the minister, who asked Calvin if he would take her to be his wife. He said he would, and then, when she was asked, she said, "I do." She reached into her bodice while the minister declared "By the power vested in me," and when Calvin leaned forward to kiss her, she slipped a knife between his ribs and watched him gasp and twitch and fall to his knees while his mouth trickled blood.

"Till death do us part," she said.

• • •

Calvin was shivering. The air was chill; his pants were wet; and all he could smell was piss. He was trying to look anywhere but at the old man's shotgun, but his eyes kept returning to it. The two barrels seemed impossibly wide, like empty eyes, hiding a darkness blacker than the black metal. He wished he could have followed Shep.

He glanced at Mr. Nowlen's eyes, which were boring into his skull whether he looked at them or not.

"I um." His face was flushed, his mouth contorting. He didn't know why he was still alive. "I don't know why."

Mr. Nowlen sighed, blowing out his cheeks. "All right, then. Let's start with *what*. *What* did you do?"

Calvin tried not to betray his surprise that Mr. Nowlen didn't already know. "W-what did Lissy say?"

"Never mind that. I'm asking you."

He tried to imagine Lissy covering for him, leaving out the worst of it, but the shotgun suggested she hadn't, while leaving unanswered the question of why it hadn't been fired. He took a deep breath and decided, provisionally, on the truth. "I. I hid in her closet. I. I don't. I." He took another, quavering breath and held it. "I guess it started at supper."

He was staring at the ground again, but a sudden movement from Mr. Nowlen made him flinch. The old man was taking off his shirt, like his father so often did when preparing to administer a beating. But instead the shirt landed in his lap. He looked up at Mr. Nowlen, confused.

"Go ahead and take off your pants. You can use my shirt to keep your legs warm." He was speaking to his own lap, no longer meeting Calvin's eyes.

As quickly as he could, Calvin stood and peeled off his pants, used the dry parts to wipe the pungent moisture from his legs, then laid them out over a branch. With one more awkward glance at Mr. Nowlen, he sat back down and covered his legs with the shirt.

"Thanks," he muttered. He didn't want to say any more, but he dreaded the sound of the old man's voice croaking at him to continue, so he forced himself to speak.

"We were kind of playing footsie under the table."

There—he could describe it as a mutual thing, Lissy a willing participant—but again his glance strayed to the shotgun. *I can do whatever I want. Nothing matters.* The truth would be easier than coming up with a lie.

"Um. So. Yeah. I was. After you left, I um, went upstairs, and, uh, hid. In Lissy's closet."

. . .

Æthel had never liked the dog, had always felt threatened by him as she sat defenseless in the vast, breezeless nest with her wings pinioned while the humans blocked its entrance. So while the dog ran from her attack, Æthel let her rage increase and feed upon itself, such that she was prepared to inflict severe injury upon the creature—except that he was surprisingly fast and agile, and she quickly grew tired. She alit upon a branch and watched with satisfaction as the dog continued to flee.

But only for a moment. When he stopped and failed to see her swooping toward him, he retraced his steps until he spotted her, uttered one hoarse, impenetrable hoot, then ducked and ran. Æthel looked the other way dismissively, too tired to pursue, her mercurial rage already spent. The vivid greens and browns of daylight signaled it was time for sleep, and she was still exhausted, but the dog was back, taunting her, feinting and weaving below her, like. Like what?

Æthel remembered the time—so long ago it now seemed—when she had wanted to join the frolics of the daytime birds, how they had mobbed her, tearing at her feathers with their tiny beaks. She remembered her sorrow, the feelings of shock and betrayal she had experienced at their misunderstanding of her intent, and a sudden intuition—a burst of hope—rose up within her. Could this dog be inviting her to play?

His long, flat tongue was spilling from his mouth in a most ridiculous fashion, and his useless tail waved back and forth as though with a mind of its own. Æthel knew little of the canine language, but these did not appear to be signs of aggression or intended predation or even fear. She raised her wings.

The dog took off again, and Æthel, despite her weariness, leaped into the air. Weaving through trees, forever on the verge of contact, she pursued the creature until her strength was entirely spent. She landed on a rock and watched her quarry recede. For a moment the dog was lost to sight, but then he reappeared, running toward her at breakneck speed. In spite of the suspected friendship, a surge of terror washed over her, and she churned the slippery air. Failing to gain any altitude, she skimmed the ground as fast as she could. Behind her, the dog's paws pounded the earth, and his rasping breath seemed all around, so she angled her flight, to catch a backward glimpse, but her wingtip caught on something—a sapling, perhaps—and a bolt of pain flashed through her—her injured wing. Suddenly she was tumbling helplessly along the forest floor, and the dog was upon her, slavering jaws agape.

* * *

Ed just wanted it to stop. He wanted to plead with Calvin to stop describing in excruciating detail how he had attacked little Lissy, the granddaughter that had been born only a few short years ago. He could picture her more easily as a toddler than an adolescent. It was obscene. There were no words. He wanted it to stop.

But listening was his penance for failing her.

Pitilessly, the boy continued, pausing here and there, sifting through his words, trying to avoid telling the worst of it, but Ed could fill in the blanks well enough. As if he were describing a scene from a movie, Calvin was saying, "I don't know if she meant to scratch me, but she got me good on the cheek here, but after that she just. She was kind of just . . . went limp and. Old Shep was scratching at the door like he was trying to dig a tunnel, but. I've never done anything like that before. I mean, I've had sex before, it's just. She's a real nice girl, and. but then, when I finished it was all of a sudden like. Like I didn't know why I'd. What I'd been thinking, I just. And I knew I had to leave before you got home, because . . . you know." He indicated the shotgun with his head. "I didn't think Shep would. Or you. I mean. I guess I thought you'd never be able to catch up with me, but, you know, also, I mean. I mean, it's not like I really hurt her or anything, it was more I just"

Ed interrupted him with a howl.

• • •

At the sound of a great beast's wail, Æthel's pursuer froze. In an instant he was running toward that horrible sound, and an instant later, Æthel was alone.

The cry had taken the wind out of her, filled her with a dread that was greater even than her fear of canine teeth. It reminded her, strangely, of the awful sound that had once issued from her own beak, and the answer that had come in the form of an eagle. The dog was like the eagle, and the beast, she realized, was the oldest human, expressing a pain that was possibly more awful than her own had been. And yet, the dread fell away as she pondered the similarity, for it emphasized the fact that she had found three friends—two eagles and a dog—predators all—who ran toward another's calamity, and one who would even play with her.

Æthel stood on the pine-needley ground, shook all her feathers out—the pain in her wing already receding—and savored a feeling of contentment more profound than any meal. In that moment, she wanted nothing more than to put down roots, lift branches, and contemplate the fullness of her heart for the rest of her life.

* * *

Ed had assumed he was already acquainted with sorrow, but Calvin's story pierced parts of his soul he hadn't known existed. He wasn't aware he was howling until he ran out of breath. He buried his head in his hands and would not stop shaking. Gone were any thoughts of vengeance or punishment. He was simply impaled, sliding helplessly down the shaft of some great lance.

"I ought to kill you," he said, softly, weakly. "I truly ought to kill you and leave your body for the crows."

When at last his hands grew aware of the stubble on his cheeks, he looked up. Shep was sitting before him, looking sideways, tongue lolling, eyes empty. He stared at the dog and said, "I can't stand to put my eyes on you, but if you know what's good for you, you'll follow me home." With that, he stood. His back wouldn't let him stand straight, so he started walking as he was—stooped, crooked, old. He used the shotgun as a cane, pushing the barrel into the earth with every other step.

His mind was blank, scoured raw by Calvin's story. The knowledge weighed him down, made every step an effort, but he was in no mood to indulge his body's protests. He plodded on, prepared to walk until the pain annealed his grief and failure. Alas, in less than an hour, he reached his yard. Shep was already at the door, waiting for Ed to let him in, which he did, but he did not hold the door open behind him. The pettiness of the gesture disturbed him. Over his shoulder he growled, "Sit yourself down in the living room and stay there."

The suspicion that there was no one behind him lasted only an instant before the screen door opened and closed again. He retrieved the phone book and looked up Frank's number. Without bothering to wonder what he would say, he poked the numbers into the phone.

"Hello?" said a voice.

"Frank?" he said.

"Just a sec."

He heard a door close. "Dad, it's for you."

"Yeah?" said Frank, after a minute.

"Frank, it's Ed Nowlen down on Maple Road. I've got your son here."

"Nonsense. My son just handed me the phone."

"Your other son. Calvin."

"Only got the one. Anyone else giving you trouble I'd suggest you call the police. Wouldn't mind getting my dog back, though."

"He assaulted my granddaughter, Frank."

There was a pause. As it stretched, Ed closed his eyes. *Was this any time for games?*

"Yep. Sounds like the cops are your best bet."

Ed hung up the phone. He had no anger left, but no patience either. He remembered that Frank's wife—Calvin's mother—had died under mysterious circumstances. He paused for only an instant to consider how often parents get away clean while their children end up in jail, then read the sticker on the base of the phone and dialed the non-emergency number for the police. The man who answered sounded brisk—efficient—and Ed was grateful.

"No emergency," he said, "but I've got a rapist here I'd like you to collect."

. . .

Shep licked the dirt from the pads of his feet. He was tired all over, yet a glow remained from his healing at the foot of the stairs and from the satisfaction of a job well done. Good's only praise had been to claim him as his own, but it was enough, as always.

He was on the verge of sleep when he heard cars in the driveway, and the whomping sound they made when people got in and out of them. He lurched to his feet and barked at the door.

"Easy, Shep," said Good from the Livingroom, but Shep heard footsteps, followed by an imperious knocking on the door that was unmistakably a threat. He lunged forward, assuring whoever was outside that he was equal to the task of defending his home.

"Shep! Lie down!"

Good was walking toward the door and Shep appraised him, to be sure he was aware of the magnitude of the threat. Good looked tired, bent like a snow-covered branch, but grim and capable, so Shep held his tongue.

When Good opened the door, three strangely-accoutred men walked in. Each of them were bigger than Good, and Shep and Good were no match for the three of them at once, but their attention was focused on the Livingroom. They seemed nervous and pawed their hips in an odd gesture that Shep had never seen before. One of them detached from his waist a set of two small collars no bigger than the neck of a cat, joined by a short chain. Good stayed in the Kitchen while the three men disappeared. He heard them issue commands, presumably to Son, who emerged a few moments later with his front paws behind his back and his head down.

One of the men was guiding him by the shoulder, another was opening the door for him, and one stayed behind to talk to Good. After a moment, the two of them left and clomped upstairs, and Shep returned to his blanket.

When the door opened again, Shep eyed suspiciously the man who was letting himself back in. He tried to decided whether a bark was in order, or maybe an intimidating growl, but the man simply closed the door behind him and looked around. When his eyes met Shep's, he stretched his lips the way humans do sometimes and walked toward him. Shep stood up in a hurry, but the man slowed down, held out his hand and fell into a crouch. His fingers were curled down, not up, so no treat, but no threat, either. Shep sniffed the fingers. There were a lot of unfamiliar smells there, but the man underneath seemed okay. He allowed the fingers to scratch under his ears, then laid back down and closed his eyes. The man stroked his head, then his footsteps withdrew and he tromped up the stairs.

Shep sighed heavily, grateful to be alone but bothered by the hubbub.

Before long, the footsteps returned, and the men passed by in single file. They went through the door and Shep listened to the whomps and growls that signaled their departure. A little while later, Good came downstairs, walked straight to where Shep was lying, and knelt down before him. Shep thumped the floor with his tail as Good placed his forehead against Shep's and his hand upon Shep's neck, kneading and rubbing. Incongruously, drops of warm rain were falling on Shep's snout.

"Good dog," he said. "You're a good dog, Shep." Then he stood and shuffled back upstairs.

At last Shep closed his heavy eyes, thought, *I'm Good dog* and fell asleep.

In his dream, Good is chasing him around the Kitchen, though whether for harm or play, he can't quite tell. Good pounces, enveloping him with his limbs, and Shep is surprised to discover that Good is a little boy. As they tumble, they merge, becoming a new kind of creature, who leaves the Kitchen to stand in the night-cool grass. A familiar scent beckons, and they prick up their ears. With a bark that reminds them of birdsong and trumpets, they bound into the forest as one.

31.

It's going to be okay, *says a voice in Lissy's head.*

Easy for you to say, *says Lissy, also inside her head.*

You have done well, *says the voice.*

What? *says Lissy.*

She woke up and tried to search the room without opening her eyes. Was mom still there? She listened for the sound of breathing, but all she could hear was a faint ringing in her ears. She risked a peek through her lashes. Her room was dim, with but a hint of daylight behind the curtains. It felt like early morning.

Day two.

She swung her legs off the edge of the bed. With difficulty, she heaved herself into a sitting position, feeling as though she'd run a marathon. Calvin's face swum before her, and she stifled a scream. It was just her imagination, but how could she ever again feel confident that she was safe and alone, even in her own room? She touched her groin and closed her eyes. Maybe, if she never thought about it ever again, she'd be okay. Just pretend it never happened.

But then, she'd also have to forget that Shep tried to rescue her, never again recall Grandpa's tears, or the voice that told her everything was going to be okay.

She touched her throat, and suddenly her whole body clenched, as though her muscles were trying to snap her bones. At the same time, she was retching like there was a road-killed porcupine in her stomach. She couldn't breathe. She slid off her bed and writhed helplessly on the floor. With tremendous effort, she rolled onto her hands and knees. Spittle hung from her lips, and her face was boiling hot. At last she got enough breath in her lungs to moan and mewl and gag, but not too loudly—she didn't want to wake her mom.

• • •

Mary shambled into the kitchen to make breakfast. She didn't really see the point, but someone had to make breakfast. Life goes on, even after you've failed at it, and traumatized daughters need bacon and eggs. The long fatty strips shriveled and pick-pock-pocked, stewing in their own juices. One of them was looking at her, so she turned it over. Onto its face *dear God*. She watched it twitch, then picked up a hen's precious infant, cracked its skull against the lip of the fry pan and tipped its tender yellow brain into the empty space beside the tortured bacon.

Over easy. Sunny side up. Such cheerful words for kidnap and murder. Nothing's ever over easy. Ovary, sí.

"Lissy, breakfast!" she called.

She wasn't expecting the usual tromp, clomp and stomp, but the utter silence was unnerving. Considering her own mood, how much more difficult would it be for Lissy to drag herself out of bed ever again? Nevertheless, she prodded the eggs and bacon onto a plate with her spatula, and felt a measure of relief when she heard footsteps descending the stairs. They were slow, and oddly paced, but they were proof of life.

Mary braced herself for whatever came next. Would Lissy be carrying an axe? Was it only boys who felt the need to kill their dads? What did Elektra do to her mom? She couldn't remember the story.

She tightened her grip on the fry pan, but Lissy turned the corner unarmed, approached the table and said, "Thanks, Mom." She put an odd stress on the first word—almost like she meant it. Their eyes met for half a moment, and she could have sworn her daughter smiled. The kitchen was starting to spin. She raised the pan and placed it in the sink, ran water over it, waited for the knife Lissy would thrust into her kidneys.

"How. Are you feeling, sweetie? Your face looks flushed; do you have a fever?"

"I'm okay. A little . . . sore, I guess."

Suddenly, the relief she felt was overwhelming. Was it possible that Lissy didn't blame her for everything? She turned, put both her hands on Lissy's head and kissed the hair between them. She took a single moment—knowing it was likely to be brief—to savor the fact that her daughter was still functioning, then turned back and pulled the fry pan out of the sink. She had forgotten to make any for herself.

"Mom?"

"Yes, dear?"

"Did all this happen because I disobeyed you? Like that time—I know it sounds stupid, but remember that time I went sledding after you told me not to? I mean, not that, exactly, but . . . is this what happens when kids don't honor their parents?"

A surge of anger made Mary lift the pan and slam it into the stove. She turned to Lissy, whose stare betrayed neither shock nor fear but only a grim determination to accept the hard truth. "Melissa Chrysanthemum Peabody, I don't know much, but I know that what happened to you was Not. Your. Fault. Do you hear me?"

"Yes, Mom," said Lissy.

• • •

Kyron awoke to a wave of pain. It was the same pain that had been ebbing and flowing throughout his tortured sleep, but this was the first time it had disengaged itself from dreams. Over and over he had dreamed he was falling, alone in a grayness like mist. At other times a warm weight had enveloped him, like his mother but with a different—yet still familiar—smell, rocking him back and forth like driftwood on the ocean.

He was empty. He had nothing left. Yet he tasted snake, and his belly was full. It was his muscles that were empty, and his brain and his heart that had nothing left to give. He was content to live or die, and had been for some time, but now, for better or for worse, he was beginning to lean toward life.

. . .

Ed woke up disoriented and immediately regretted waking up at all. His teeth were clenched. His whole body was drawn up into a ball as tight as a fist. In fact, his hands were the only part of him that weren't. He tried to stretch out one leg and immediately regretted that, as well. He was a wreck. Every muscle ached, and none worse than his heart. Ever since he'd gone to bed after the police left, he had clambered up and down the mountain, often on his hands and knees, searching for something he couldn't remember or fleeing from something he couldn't see. He was shocked to realize that it was somehow the following morning. Never in his life had he slept so long. And yet, part of him wanted nothing more than to continue his fruitless quest for oblivion. The only reason not to was that Shep would be just as wrecked and would need food and water and a chance to pee somewhere other than the kitchen floor.

"Bad dog," he croaked.

It took some time, but he managed to push and pull his limbs parallel with his torso. From there it was a relatively simple matter to swing his legs off the edge of the bed and sit up. Simple but painful. He groaned as he stood, pulled his trousers on and gingerly negotiated the stairs.

Before he reached the bottom step, he sensed that the silence was too profound. His mind raced. Had Shep come in with him yesterday? Had one of the police officers let him out? He stopped in the living room and called out, "Shep?"

He waited for a sign, a thump from Shep's tail, or a scratch at the door. He inhaled a thick lungful of dread and walked into the kitchen.

To his great relief, Shep was lying in his usual spot by the woodstove. "Are you feeling as wretched as me?" he asked as he walked to the stove, bent down, and cuffed the dog gently on his rump.

His brain couldn't process it. Shep's rump was cold and immobile. He stayed bent over, frozen, searching for some way to reinterpret the evidence.

"Shep?" he said at last. "Shep?"

A tear fell on the dog's back, and finally he knew. He fell to his knees and a part of him kept falling, through the floor and into the cool, dark bowels of the earth. He put his arms awkwardly around the last of his household to depart. He pressed his cheek to the back of the dog's neck, and when the head shifted sickeningly, he recoiled. Shep was gone; he was hugging a corpse. He stood up and wiped his sleeve across his eyes.

The soreness of his muscles was unimportant—a background detail. "Damn it, Shep. Damn you." He shook his head, more like palsy than denial. Glancing at the ceiling, he knew it would be better not to wait. He took a few quick breaths, closed his eyes briefly, then leaned over to pick up the too-big body and carry it awkwardly to the door. Somehow he managed to turn the knob and squeeze through the doorway like a groom bearing his bride but in the wrong direction. He walked to the spot—not far from the swing—where Shep had comforted him after his fall, and—without giving himself time to think—deposited the body and went to the shed for a shovel.

From time to time as he worked, he'd glance at his old friend's remains and wonder where he'd gone. Memories came of the night's adventure, of Shep's strange vitality, of his boundless energy, but mostly the glimpses his mind provided were of previous times—Shep's life flashing before his eyes. Some of the memories included Karen or Mary or Lissy, and he would momentarily be confused about who he was burying.

The work required no effort. He wondered if he were dreaming, but only for an instant. Time was passing, his muscles were working, there were rocks in the soil that had to be dug around and pulled out by hand. Worms writhed in the edges of the pit, and the birds would not stop whistling.

When the hole was big enough, he heaved the dog-shaped mass into it, gave himself just enough time to let his mouth frown with grief, then pushed the pile of dirt and rocks back in.

He would mark it later, maybe even say a few words, but for now it was all he could do to return the shovel to the shed and himself to the kitchen without shattering like a dropped glass.

· · ·

For the third time in two days, the maple tree wept, after the manner of trees, in silence and stillness, feeling as though a stiff winter gale were pelting her with frozen rain.

· · ·

Lissy knew Mom would worry if she left the house without telling her, but she also knew that if she waited for the words to come—the words that would sufficiently explain the sudden impulse to her mother—she'd never leave, and for some reason she needed to be outside, so she closed the door quietly behind her and stepped into the garage. Then she unlocked the side door and stepped into the sunshine of a bright, midsummer morning. Halfway down the driveway she stopped, as though a hand had been placed on her shoulder, and she braced herself, convinced that the voice from this morning would insist she inform her mother of her whereabouts. Instead came a memory of Moses from Sunday school. With the slightest of shrugs she toed off her shoes and stepped into the dew-glistening grass.

She imagined herself running, skipping, cartwheeling back and forth across the lawn, but joy was yet a long ways off. This was simply a time to feel the chill dew on her bare feet and the clumps in the sod. It was time to breathe deep and notice the sparks in the lilac bushes where the sun glanced off dewdrops at just the right angle. It was time to listen to the cardinal's three note crescendo and the mourning dove's hollow lament.

"*Ow*," she said.

"I mean, thank you for all this and everything, but *ow*.

"Just. *Ow*."

* * *

The guard who opened the door was overweight, moving slowly, and breathing heavily. "All right," he said, and Calvin stood. He wondered if he should offer his wrists for cuffs but the guard simply took his arm with a surprisingly strong grip and guided him out of the cell.

The narrow hallway smelled of disinfectant, almost like a hospital, and echoed their every footstep. They passed through three locked doors to get out of the cell block, and as he passed through the last one, he felt a weight lift. It was the weight of confinement that he would almost certainly get used to over the coming years. His heart lurched at the thought, but he took a deep breath and tried to resign himself to it, even as tears sprang into his eyes. He wondered if he would break down and cry, his knees buckling so that the guard would have to drag him. The thought was almost funny.

The counselor didn't look up when they entered. He was shuffling papers from a folder on the table in front of him. The guard dropped Calvin's arm and grabbed a metal folding chair from among those that lined the walls, dragged it to the table, placed a hand on Calvin's shoulder and pushed him down into it. He sat down heavily and the guard withdrew, but Calvin could sense his presence behind him as though the hand were still on his shoulder.

The counselor still hadn't looked up from his papers. Calvin tried to read them, but the words looked like gibberish upside down, and his eyes wouldn't focus. The whole situation felt unreal. His past—the life that he had lived before and everything that he had ever done or said or thought—seemed to belong to someone else. It was as though he had just now come into existence.

At last the counselor looked up.

"Why don't you tell me why you're here, Mr. Berman?" he said.

Calvin closed his eyes and thought about the conversation he'd had with Mr. Nowlen on the mountainside. About all the things he wished he'd said.

"Well. . . . my mom committed suicide." He didn't mean it as an excuse, but he knew immediately that it sounded like one. He glanced at the piercing eyes. They didn't waver.

"But then," he continued, hurriedly. "My brother was saying . . . kept telling me that nothing mattered. Like . . . like whatever you did . . . you could do anything at all, and it wouldn't matter, because . . ." He wanted to pause and think, but he didn't want to give the counselor a chance to respond until he'd finished his thought. "So I was experimenting, sort of. Like. I don't know, testing my brother's hypothesis, you know? I didn't mean to . . . hurt anyone."

"But you did," said the counselor.

Calvin stared at those eyes. A wave was rising up within him, the crest of an overwhelming emotion. *Oh, look*, he said to himself, *A real emotion*. As he expected, the wave subsided, but though he was a little disappointed, as always, it at least provided him with a touchstone—proof that he was still himself: the boy with no emotions. "Yeah. I guess so," he said.

"And did it matter?"

Calvin hesitated, shocked by the gentleness with which the counselor had asked. He thought about it, remembered the terror in Lissy's eyes, his hand around her throat. Temporarily unable to speak, he nodded once, then his mouth contracted into a frown and he nodded more emphatically. Tears fell from his eyes, and his shoulders started quaking. Snorting noises issued from his throat and sinuses. He could no longer see through the steady stream of tears. And then all thought was obliterated under an avalanche of raw emotion, and all he knew was that he could not stop nodding.

"Yeah," said the counselor.

· · ·

Corwynn had been staring at her love all morning. Now that the sun was high, he no longer needed her warmth, so she sat a little apart from him and stared, particularly at the odd scar on his beak. The owl, sleeping in the shade of leaves not far away, had brought them an assortment of mice and shrews and voles. Enough to last a couple of days, so there was no need to hunt. In the bright sunlight there was no need to guard. So she stared at Kyron's supine form and did nothing else at all.

When her youngest alit on a nearby branch, Corwynn shifted her gaze for only a moment, received his acknowledgment—noting with satisfaction his health and strength—then returned her attention to Kyron. The same when her eldest touched down. The sun was nearly directly overhead when her daughter arrived and flagrantly failed to acknowledge her. It was hard to believe, on such a perfect day, that she could be hurt by a petty lack of respect, but she wanted to rise up and flap her wings in protest.

But then Kyron shifted, as if sensing that the time had come. He opened his eyes and, after a moment's searching, found hers. Corwynn felt a release, blinked languorously, and let her hurt feelings, her umbrage, the burden of her former despair and all her gormless fears just waft away.

Her daughter chittered a welcome to a father she had never seen before, and Corwynn heard a rustle from the foliage where the owl was concealed. As if agreeing that the time of danger was finally over, the owl circled the aerie once, then floated silently away.

32.

It was almost lunchtime on the third day after Lissy's return when Mary decided to pick up where she'd left off with her Bible study. She needed wisdom, comfort, and advice, all things the Bible was supposed to provide. But, of course, the bookmarks still opened to "The Command to Sacrifice Isaac," so at long last she read the passage. It was difficult to get through the whole story, because she kept interrupting it with questions.

Why didn't you argue? It had been weeks since she'd read the prior passages, but she was sure she remembered Abraham arguing with God in case there might be ten righteous people left in Sodom. Yet he didn't object at all when God commanded him to sacrifice his promised son.

And when his son asked him where the sacrifice was, how could he answer with such seeming serenity?

How could he ask his son to carry the wood for the fire without screaming at God to relent?

The obvious answer to all these questions—the conclusion she felt certain she was supposed to draw—was that Abraham had learned to trust God in every circumstance, but she didn't buy it.

The study guide pointed to the book of Hebrews, which claimed that Abraham had expected Isaac to rise from the dead. And that was exactly the sort of wisdom, comfort, and advice Mary was looking for, but—wasn't three days the accepted timeframe for resurrection? And what would that even look like? Was Lissy going to suddenly wake up one day and be her usual surly teenage self again? Mary tried to project down the decades—would she be okay in her twenties, her thirties, her eighties? It seemed clear that Lissy would never trust another human being again, never feel safe, never . . .

It would be so much easier if she could blame God or Dad or Fate for offering Lissy up to that that shit-headed ass-wipe's lust, but the fault was incontrovertibly her own. She had failed the most fundamental test of parenthood by forsaking her child.

Clearly, she ought to have sacrificed herself in Lissy's stead, continuing to surrender her own happiness and fulfillment in favor of Lissy's. Maybe then, when she was beaten down by her own inadequacies and whatever onslaughts of teenage rage, an angel might have stepped between them and said "Mary! Now I know that you love me, for you have not withheld yourself, your only self, from your daughter." Or something.

At this point, any possible alternative was moot. She had failed her daughter, and the flaming sword of the irrevocable past prevented her from ever taking it back.

. . .

Æthel, at long last returning to her old hollow tree, pulled up short and perched in a lower branch of a pine. From within the dark cavity of the entrance to her home, the eyes of a red squirrel peered out at her. On the ground below, a second squirrel raced for the trunk and scampered up the bark. When it reached the hole, it stopped and twisted its head around to face her, its front feet spread straight in front of it, chittering in a most aggressive yet pathetically unthreatening way. Æthel cocked her head and considered the best angle of attack. The first face never moved; it was breathing rapidly but shallowly, its whiskers drooping.

Æthel cocked her head in the other direction. Both squirrels ought to be cowering as deep inside her abandoned home as possible. She would be hard pressed to oust them within the confines of the hollow. Instead, one challenged her while the other simply stared. She drew her head backward as it occurred to her that the squirrel inside was sick. Indeed, she saw that it was near death, and would not be so difficult to remove after all, yet doubt cast a shadow on her mind.

In the last few days, Æthel had killed a possum, a dove, three mice, and a fish. All had been laid in the aerie but the mice, which she had swallowed herself, remembering each time that her throat was a burrow. And indeed it would be better to welcome the sick squirrel home to her gullet, then to let it suffer through its last few days—if only the healthy squirrel's bravado didn't remind her so strongly of her friends. She twisted her head around backwards and closed her eyes.

At last she untwisted her neck to face the usurpers. The chitterer never flinched as she leaped towards it, brushed a wingtip along the length of its body and flew away.

Surely the forest had other hollow trees.

                                            ◦ ◦ ◦

Ed wanted to hit something. He wanted to get into a fist fight, straddle someone's chest, and pummel their face until his knuckles bled.

Instead, he was standing in the middle of his dead-end dirt road, smoking. His dog was dead, his houseguests gone, his heart in pieces, and he couldn't take any of it back, and he couldn't take a single step forward. He was stuck in the middle of the road, and he only had five more cigarettes.

"Lord," he said, his voice hoarse but not uncertain. "I've given it a lot of thought over the years, especially lately." He nodded, then shook his head. "And I've finally decided that you can go fuck yourself."

His throat constricted with emotion and tears began to rise, but he snarled at them until they fled. "Yep."

He coughed, spat, pulled out another cigarette, but, before he could light it, he was startled by a noise—something big was crashing toward him. Instinctively, he planted his feet, bent his knees, and raised his walking stick. What emerged from the underbrush at the side of the road was a scrawny, mud-caked dog that stopped short at the sight of Ed, backed up a couple paces, and wagged its tail between its legs.

Moving slowly, Ed stretched out his hand and settled into a crouch, carefully balancing on one knee. His hip barely winced.

"Well, hey there, pup," he said. "What's your name?"

The dog held back, but its nose strained forward, trying to draw the smells from Ed's outstretched fingers into its nostrils. Its eyes shifted continuously from Ed's hand to his eyes, betraying a clear admixture of fear and longing.

"It's okay," Ed said, raising his voice an octave and gentling it as best he could. "I'm not going to hurt you."

At last the dog took a tentative step, then another. Ed remembered that he probably still had a dog biscuit or two in his pockets. When he pulled his hand away to check, the dog waddled backwards. For a moment it looked ready to bolt, but, when Ed tossed the biscuit at its feet, it snatched the treat up and nearly swallowed it whole. Ed held another in his hand, and soon enough the dog stepped forward to take it and suffered himself to be petted while he ate it.

"There's a good dog," he said. "Who's a good dog?"

Autumn

33.

BILLY JENSEN POKED THE GROUND WITH A STICK. WHEN THE GROUND FAILED to react, he pushed harder and gave the stick a twist. Faintly, he heard the earth scream—a cacophony made up of thousands of voices. Almost lost in the din were the screams of his parents. It was really only in the wee hours (as Gran called the middle of the night), when he couldn't sleep, that he recalled them clear—hanging upside down from the road, howling his name as he sat in the car, his seatbelt painfully tight, as another car, also upside down, scraped his parents away. Later he would learn that the people in the car were friends with the first drunk driver who had sped around the same dangerous curve in the wrong lane and . . .

He lived with Gran now, who often sent him out to play in the yard. Billy's idea of playing was to sit in the swing his great-great-grandfather had made and poke the ground with a stick.

His great-grandmother was visiting today, which meant he had to stay out of her way. Nanana didn't like boys. Mom used to say it had something to do with what happened to Gran a long time ago, but he'd never heard any details. It was funny though, because if Nanana was mad at boys because of something that happened to Gran, then why did Gran love him so much? She was the one who sat with him after the Crash. Just sat and held his hand and never asked him what he was thinking or feeling. There had never been any question in his mind that Gran's would be where he would live from now on.

Nanana was old. He didn't think any of his friends had great-grandmothers. She walked slow, hunched over, and there was always spittle in the corner of her mouth. She had warmed to him only slightly after the Crash. Her sympathy was grudging, but it helped. Every little thing helped—at least a little. What bothered him was how Nanana treated Gran.

Gran was the strongest and best person he knew. She always knew what to say, even when that something was nothing at all. And also, she was fearless. She'd stood up to a bear, once—no fooling. They'd snuck up on it while walking through the woods. They hadn't meant to, of course, but Gran never liked sticking to trails. It was lying in a patch of tall grass, curled up like a cat in a sunbeam. Whenever Gran told the story (which wasn't nearly often enough, in Billy's opinion), she said that it had probably eaten something that didn't agree with it, and that's why it was sleeping in the middle of the day, and also why it didn't eat them right away.

All Billy knew was that a monster rose up before him, its mouth wide and groaning, but he barely had time to be frightened before Gran was screaming at it to go away, fists balled at her side, leaning forward, just a few feet away from a hairy beast that was head and shoulders taller than her. It had leaned backward, away from her face, and Billy didn't blame it. He had never seen such a scary expression as the one Gran wore except once in a movie. When it was leaning too far to balance, it twisted around and took off on all fours in the opposite direction.

The tension between Nanana and Gran was somehow the opposite of the bear story. With Nanana it was Gran who shied away. Not like she was scared, but more like a wise old dog would slink away from a skunk. Although Nanana smelled funny, it was nowhere near as bad as a skunk, and Billy could tell that

Nanana's feelings were hurt every time, but Gran, who could make friends with anyone, for some reason shrank a little whenever Nanana started talking.

When he was younger he assumed it was because Nanana was hard to understand, but as he got older and spent more time with her, he learned how to listen to her, and realized that it was more *what* she said than how she said it.

Thinking about what Nanana might be saying to Gran right now made him drop the stick, leave the swing, and trot toward the house. When he slipped into the kitchen, Gran gave him one of the cookies Nanana had brought. Nanana gave him a sour smile. Their conversation was about like he'd expected.

"Mom," said Gran. "Sit down. You're making me nervous."

"Don't tell me to sit down; you sit down. I'm fine where I am."

"You're not fine; I can see the pain in your face."

"It's my pain; I'll carry it how I like."

"You're impossible."

"I'm your mother."

Gran pursed her lips and looked away, but Billy couldn't tell what she was looking at.

"Don't look at me like that," said Nanana.

"I'm not looking at you," said Gran.

"Well, stop it. I did the best I could."

Gran blew out her cheeks and raised her eyebrows comically.

"For crying out loud, Mom; it's been— Now it's been fifty years. You officially win the award for not letting something go. Now let it go."

"It was your grandfather's fault. He never should have trusted that rat-faced little shit-eater."

"Mother! Please don't swear in front of Billy."

Hoping to ease the tension, Billy said "I don't care."

"Hush, child," said Gran. "I don't want to hear you using such language."

"I won't."

"No, no—he'll grow a up as polite as can be. A perfect gentleman."

"Yes, he will. There's no one sweeter than my Billy."

"Oh, he's sweet all right. Sweet as antifreeze and twice as deadly."

"Mother!"

"It doesn't help anyone to pretend otherwise."

Then Gran made a sound like growling, almost exactly like the bear had sounded, and Nanana's eyes went wide.

It was too much. He was mad at both of them, but he jumped in front of Gran, balled his fists and screamed at his favorite person in the whole world:

"Go 'way! You're scaring her! Go 'way!"

Gran was shocked into silence and, what was rarer, so was Nanana. Then they both started laughing at once. They laughed and laughed, until Billy started laughing, too.

Nanana died a few years later, but Billy would always remember her laughter.

Winter, Part 2

34.

Melissa Chrysanthemum Comstock was 93 years old, dreaming and knitting in her rocking chair in the wee hours of a sweltering summer night. She rarely went to bed anymore, even though her grandson Bill had converted the dining room into a permanent downstairs bedroom after she broke her hip. But many years earlier it had served as a temporary bedroom for an old friend and her hospice nurse, who was also an old friend, so, in Melissa's mind, it was still Beth Anne's room, and even though Jenna, too, had long since passed away, the room would always hold too many poignant memories to afford a restful slumber.

Melissa had raised her grandson after Molly and Richard were killed by a drunk driver. He had been a kind boy, always rescuing animals and befriending the friendless. His great-grandma, Melissa's mother, died when he was young, but not before he helped thaw the awkward coolness that had long separated mother and daughter. In high school and college, he had helped out in her veterinary practice. Now he was a therapist who specialized in addictions.

The cat, Mysty, pounced on the ball of yarn then leaped away and rehid beneath the couch. It hardly startled her anymore.

Bill had moved in on her 90th birthday, not long after his divorce. He had said he needed a place to stay, and he always joked to visitors that he was shamelessly mooching off his grandmother, but he could just as easily have committed her to a nursing home and had the house to himself.

During the summer months, Bill's daughter, Kiki, stayed with them. The girl was upstairs now, in Melissa's old bedroom, the one she still thought of as belonging to her own grandparents. Bill was in the guest room. The room in-between was full of old boxes and stacks of magazines, a broken stationary bike, and an antique electric organ. Once or twice a week she had used to sit there and play old hymns. That's what she missed most about the upstairs now that her hip precluded climbing.

The sound of a creaking floorboard upstairs made her clutch her chest.

It's just Kiki, she told herself, but her heart was hammering, a film of sweat erupted from her forehead and she felt short of breath. Another creak: Kiki was trying to be quiet, but the slowness of her steps did nothing but attenuate the high-pitched groan.

It was too much. She pushed herself upright, limped through the kitchen and stepped outside, where a breeze cooled her forehead and the feeling of openness unconstricted her chest. The stars glittered in all their ridiculous profusion, and the quiet rustling of leaves slowed her heart.

She drew a deep breath and let it out slow. "You're okay," she told herself. "You're safe."

Decades of therapy, and that's what she had to show for it: Positive self talk.

The moon had yet to rise—starlight and dim air-glow were the only illumination—but as her eyes adjusted, it was enough. Bears didn't scare her, though several had been sighted recently, and crazed axe murderers were rare in these parts. An owl hooted, and a coyote answered—a familiar conversation.

She had not thought to bring a cane, and her hip was already beginning to ache, but she wasn't yet ready to go back inside. Kiki's plastic tire swing dangled dimly from the gnarled maple, but it was not a tempting seat. The front steps would be better, but she didn't want her back that close to the house. Likewise the barn was a poor option, if only because it was falling apart. She didn't want to be inside of anything right now. What she wanted was to lie down in the grass and stargaze. She knew that the dew would seep through her clothes, that there would be inconveniently placed lumps and probably bugs that would get in her hair, but

Oh, what the hell.

She lowered herself awkwardly onto her hands and knees and rolled over. With her legs pointing toward the house, she dropped her head into the grass, closed her eyes, and let all the tension in her body leech into the earth. It was a lengthy process, but when it was finished, the ground beneath her felt as warm as a blanket, and she opened her eyes to be amazed anew at the shimmering chiaroscuro of distant suns.

Once her tension dissipated, she let her mind go empty as well. When the image came to her of a little old lady lying primly on her back in her dark front yard, she refused to laugh at it—not because it wasn't funny, or because she felt any sense of dignity—but because she wanted to continue lying there unselfconsciously. Empty. Just another point of consciousness in a living world.

Are you there? she asked.

As usual, there was no specific response, but she didn't mind. The slightest stirring in her heart might have been an answer, but then again maybe not. So hard to tell.

Perhaps an hour passed before the ground grew uncomfortable and the air just a shade too cool. With a sigh, she set about the process of standing up. She wished she'd brought her cane.

In the time she had been outside, the house had released its dread, and she crossed the unlit kitchen without fear. In the living room, Kiki was asleep on the floor, the afghan from the back of the couch drawn tightly around her shoulders. Melissa let her lie, sat down in her chair and picked up her knitting. Mysty was nowhere in sight.

As the clock struck four, Kiki came awake and looked around in confusion. When she saw Melissa, she smiled without surprise and crawled over to lay her head in her great-grandmother's lap.

Such lovely trust, she thought, as she stroked Kiki's hair. *Such naive and heartbreaking trust. Another sunflower for you to plant.*

She will endure many trials and hardships, said a voice, *but also much joy and peace, and she will never be uprooted, as you were, for the ground in which I have planted you is yours. It belongs to you and to your offspring for generations to come, for you have found favor in my sight.*

Tears were in her eyes as a tingling warmth welled within her chest. "Thank you," she whispered. "Oh, *thank you.*"

The soft hair beneath her hand seemed infinitely precious, and she stilled her hand from stroking, lest her heart burst.

She was suddenly unaccountably tired. She hadn't realized that her shoulders yet retained a vestigial tension until it loosened. She closed her eyes, and let her thoughts run free. . . .

> *In her dream, she is always falling, alone in a grayness like mist. The wind, that strong, sustaining spirit, has forsaken her again. The sadness she feels is tempered by the realization that she has wings. She holds them out before her to inspect the feathers. She had assumed they would be white, like an angel's, but instead they are mottled gray and brown—strange yet familiar.*
>
> *In the absence of air, her wings are useless, and the speed of her descent increases. For a moment she fears asphyxiation, but her next breath assuages the panic. She wonders how soon she'll slam to the ground, but then she*

recalls she has been here before, and that panic has never helped, so she takes another breath, releases it, and does what has long come naturally:

She spreads out her wings, and she waits.

35.

Mysty gazes at them from the security of underneath. When she is certain they are asleep, she allows herself a luxurious blink. This one she likes. And Mama, of course. But the one above is too loud. Always roaring, "Hahahahaha!" over and over again. Scares the shit out of her. Hopefully that one will stay above until daylight, like usual. She slides out from underneath and sniffs the joint of the hind leg of the one on the floor. *Mmmmmm*, good smells. Trustworthy smells. She rubs one cheek against the joint, then the other cheek. Now they are no longer other, but one being. In their dream, they are floating through yellow and green elation with nothing to fear.

She inspects the nook between the dreaming head and Mama's torso and flicks her tail. It looks cozy there. Lightly, she leaps. In Mama's dream, she is falling, falling, falling through a slackness of grief with no one to catch her. Mysty puts one paw on Mama's breast and sniffs. She pushes her forehead against Mama's cheek, first one side, then the other. The long, gray fur from Mama's head brushes her like the lightest of tongues. Mama awakes and draws her paw down Mysty's back, and Mysty stretches into it. She licks the tip of Mama's nose before curling up and falling asleep.

All is well until daylight, when the one from above clomps down, stops in front of Mama and begins—softly at first but rapidly rising—to roar. Soon,

Mama wakes up, bares her teeth, and pants through her nose. The head on Mama's legs growls, kittenishly.

Together, they will face with courage the one who roars, but suddenly Mama's legs separate from her torso, pulling Mysty with them. No—not Mama's legs—she has been lying on the head fur of the one with whom she had bonded, who is now yowling, and Mysty is tangled. Panic erupts. Chaos consumes her.

Mysty gazes—from the farthest recesses of underneath—at the hind paws of the ones she moments before assumed were one. All three are others now, roaring together, and she alone is one, and small. She has always been alone, ever since she was stolen from First Mama and taken to the other place of rotten smells and little food and no affection. She had thought this new place was better, but she will always be alone, because snug and full and clean are tricks.

Front paws appear amongst the hind paws, followed by head fur, then eyes. This one is mewling, reaching, its front paw dancing and scratching the ground. Mysty tries to ignore it, but its contortions are provocative. Angry, she reaches her own front paw to swat it. It retreats—but not far—and is still. Then it dances again, and Mysty follows, squirming forward, intent on her prey. Together they dance until her prey ventures out from underneath. Mysty knows it is dangerous, but this prey cannot be allowed to escape. She reaches one paw out from underneath, then the other. Her prey is paralyzed with fear, so she takes her chance and pursues, only to be grasped and lifted. She tries to escape, but she has fallen for their tricks once again and this time, surely, she will be eaten for real.

Instead there is stroking, intimate and affectionate, this one and Mama and the roarer all standing close, bringing comfort. The roarer is tickling her chin, and she cannot help but purr.

Here at last is Mama, union, home.

She drowns in it.

www.ingramcontent.com/pod-product-compliance
Lightning Source LLC
Chambersburg PA
CBHW030149100526
44592CB00009B/194